HIDDEN HISTORY
of
NORTHWESTERN PENNSYLVANIA

Jessica Hilburn

THE
History
PRESS

Published by The History Press
Charleston, SC
www.historypress.com

First published 2019

Manufactured in the United States

ISBN 9781467141451

Library of Congress Control Number: 2019939730

Notice: The information in this book is true and complete to the best of our knowledge. It is offered without guarantee on the part of the author or The History Press. The author and The History Press disclaim all liability in connection with the use of this book.

For Mom, Dad and Julie. Of all the history I'll ever know, my favorite is ours.

CONTENTS

ACKNOWLEDGEMENTS

This book has been a labor of love (heavy on both labor *and* love) from the moment the idea popped into my head on New Year's Day 2018 until the final edit was made. Northwestern Pennsylvania is my home, and its history runs through my veins. I am honored to have given voice to a small percentage of its hidden stories.

First and foremost, I want to thank my family—Mom, Dad, Julie and our home of furry felines—for supporting and encouraging me, not letting me procrastinate and reinforcing my confidence in times of crisis. Thank you especially to my mom, who has been my rock, proofreader, soundboard and best friend since 1993. I love you all more than words.

To all whom I have lost—Pap, Baba, Grandpa, Grandma, Uncle Ken—I know you are so proud.

Thank you to everyone at Benson Memorial Library—especially Justin, Becky and our board of directors—for supporting this endeavor and allowing me to use content from our blog, *NWPA Stories*. You're invaluable.

A huge thank-you to my best friend, Lindsay, who was always there for texts, video chats and visits that made me feel human again and reminded me that this work is important. Thanks, Helen.

Deepest thanks to the following interviewees, archives, museums and libraries that helped me with my research and provided images for this book—I could not have done it without you: Nick Sekel, Benson Memorial Library, Drake Well Museum, the *Titusville Herald*, Erie County Public Library and Blasco Memorial Library Heritage Room. Libraries are for everyone.

Enormous thanks to my acquisitions editor, J. Banks Smither, who believed in me and this project and answered every question I had. Thank you to everyone at The History Press who turned this book from a dream into a reality. I can never express how truly thankful I am to you for making my dream come true.

A big thank-you to everyone who has been a part of my life as a historian—from Titusville High School to Mercyhurst University to Edinboro University of Pennsylvania—who fostered my creativity, encouraged exploration and helped me find my (very argumentative) voice; to Oil Region Alliance and Drake Well Museum, both of which helped me get my feet wet in this wide historical world; and everyone who has shaped me into the social servant, historian and human being I am today. I would not be who I am without you.

Ask the questions. Find the answers.

INTRODUCTION

Maybe the most important reason for writing is to prevent the erosion of time, so that memories will not be blown away by the wind. Write to register history and name each thing. Write what should not be forgotten.
—Isabelle Allende

I t's quiet here in Northwestern Pennsylvania. You can drive through our lush green hills and valleys as the cicadas sing in the summer, gaze at the bright fall leaves as they drift to earth in the peak of October, taste and touch the seemingly never-ending lake effect snow and peek at fawns emerging from the woods on a dewy May morning. But if you listen closely, you can hear the whispers of our ancestors drift through the breeze and into your ear, begging for you to look harder.

In this book, we will pull back the curtain on the hidden stories that live in our foothills. From the pioneer days of an unfettered wilderness to the hustle and bustle of industrial-era cities and towns, we will explore ghastly murders and terrible tragedies, ghostly books and political revivals. Whether spurting from the ground or arcing through the air on the way to the endzone, the hidden history of Northwestern Pennsylvania is in the details of the lives of people who lived it.

History can often be boiled down into dry events and times, forgetting the beating heart of our collective past: us. Humans are the central line to every story, every piece of hidden history. Each part will dive into a moment in our past that is not widely known. The first explores the horror that can develop in a secluded area of the country where quack doctors, untreated mental illnesses and unexplainable murders splashed across the pages of local newspapers have disappeared into the archives, only to be resurrected once again.

As industry developed and transportation grew, trains became the single most important factor tying disparate communities together across the region. Unscrupulous barons took advantage of the need for speed, allowing accident after accident to claim the lives of countless innocent passengers, horrifying their communities, while ultimately evading justice.

Next, we will step into the more unusual stories of this neck of the woods, including ghosts, asylums and gangs of fire-starters that were almost hanged in public gallows in front of a cheering crowd. As the spirits descended, early Northwestern Pennsylvanians were captivated by their allure, including a few prominent society figures who claimed to commune with the dead.

For a change of pace, the fourth chapter explores a less grisly side of our history: industrialization in steel, toymaking that made children smile for a generation, a Socialist political revival at one of the oldest exposition parks in the country and an immigrant religion that was carried on the backs of the poor to a section of Erie County marked by fields and dirt roads, not unlike the home they left in central Europe. Work, play, politics and worship are unique in Northwestern Pennsylvania, with human stories hiding around every bend.

Although a great deal of this area is known for a thick, dark substance drilled from deep in the earth, another much clearer liquid has a layered history as well. The first commercial oil well was drilled in Titusville in 1859, but mineral water did not wait long to see its own industry innovated in the area. At Cambridge Springs, Pleasantville and Corry, mineral water became the new clear gold, and people flocked to the area to try a sip of the curative waters.

Another cure people hungered for was to treat the litany of illnesses, ailments and diseases with which they were plagued throughout the nineteenth and early twentieth centuries. As a result, "cures, "remedies," "liniments" and more cropped up, as concocted by different businesses across the tri-county area. The tonics claimed to help with everything from deadly consumption to rashes and animal ailments. Traveling medicine shows were popular, giving those in the most secluded areas a tie to the world and hope for recovery. Unfortunately for them, rural medicines were usually more show than cure, leaving scores of people still knocking on death's door.

History is marked by great men. So often forgotten are the great women who shook the world yet were passed over in the written record. The seventh chapter gives voice to the stories of six women—mothers, daughters and granddaughters—who dedicated their lives to changing the status quo in any way they could: a mother and daughter from Warren who used their fortune and sadness-riddled lives to help those in need, a woman and her granddaughter from Erie who were pioneers of African American business and education and a mother and daughter from Girard who used their power to create infrastructure and stand up to none other than the president of the United States. Titans of industry, business and leadership were the women whose hidden histories are illuminated here.

Finally, we dive into a fun and inspirational set of hidden stories that call to some of our innermost drives at competition and adrenaline: sports. From the story of how the most famous award in college football finds its roots in the backyards of coopers in Titusville to an African American baseball team that showed the community why equality was essential and a racehorse that no one believed in and yet soared to new heights of triumph, Northwestern Pennsylvania guards no shortage of stories that will get your pulse pounding en route to victory.

Throughout each of these stories, you will glimpse what it was like to live in one of the most rural areas of Penn's Woods during multiple periods of boom and bust. These hidden histories allow you to live with your ancestors through times of soaring triumph and heartbreaking sorrow. By exploring our hidden history, we add color and shape to the vast picture of the past we collectively share. Our history is living and breathing. It never stopped existing simply because we forgot it was there. So, step inside, let your eyes adjust and visit the hidden history of Northwestern Pennsylvania.

Chapter 1

Horror, Bloodshed and Murder in Penn's Woods

The Jennings Horror

Mary Jennings was a sweet fifteen-year-old girl who was going to school and growing up quietly in the Northwestern Pennsylvania countryside until her life was viciously taken, to the shock and dismay of the entire region, in February 1876.

Miss Jennings was a perfectly healthy young woman when a man came to town and professed her to be ill and in need of treatment at once. J.S. Osborn declared that she was afflicted with blood cancer and must be immediately treated, to the surprise of her family and friends. The *Titusville Herald* noted, "She was a young girl just merging into womanhood, and was troubled with those disabilities incident to her age, such as occasional headache, pain in the stomach, nervousness and a general feeling of unrest. The symptoms were physiological or natural, and therefore required no medical interference. It is only necessary that they should have attended to her sanitary or hygenic [*sic*] condition to recover her in the process of time to the natural functions of her womanhood."

In layman's terms, Mary was entering puberty, getting some teenage acne and starting her period. However, Osborn was about to make sure Mary would never see the end of her teenage years.

As treatment for her "affliction," the doctor applied a corrosive salve to her skin—bichloride of mercury. The compound created horrific blisters

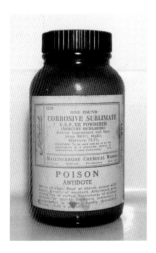

Example of a bottle of mercury bichloride, such as that killed young Mary Jennings. *Splarka, Wikimedia Commons.*

across her entire body, from her neck to the base of her spine. Osborn also rubbed it on her face and hair. Mary's entire body began to shed its own skin, sloughing off in pieces and burning her to death from the outside in. Not only did her skin come away from her body, but even her gums, teeth and internal organs began to blister and rupture. The *Herald* termed her death worse than murder.

The *Herald* reporter went on to say that there has never been "a more cruel, relentless or appalling death than that which overtook this innocent and estimable young lady, who with her body rotted to the bones died in unendurable agony, on her hands and knees, calling on her God to kill her and relieve her from the most excruciating suffering. Crucifixion is considered to be one of the most painful deaths and has been ostracized by all civilized nations, but it is nothing compared with the death of Mary Jennings. The former takes but few hours to destroy life, but the latter took three weeks of agony utterly indescribable by human pen."

Three weeks it took poor Mary Jennings to succumb to her horrific injuries. And she was not the only victim.

The *Herald* found out that Osborn was not a real doctor, but a quack who posed as a medical professional and preyed on a variety of communities across Northwestern Pennsylvania. Upon investigating, the paper uncovered that he also inflicted his hideous compound on other people across the region. A woman from Sugar Creek was dying at the same time as Mary Jennings from being mutilated by Osborn. The previous October, Osborn had also applied his liniment to a woman named Mrs. Hancox and her two sons. Before "treating" them, Osborn bled Hancox to the point of fainting and then applied the mercury across her back. He then did the same to her two sons. Fortunately, these three victims did not die due to timely intervention by a true medical professional, Dr. George Barr.

Osborn was eventually caught in Dempseytown and tried on February 9, 1876. He was imprisoned, but unfortunately his imprisonment was not permanent. The October 5, 1876 edition of the *Herald* reported that Osborn was able to flee his jail cell by applying the same corrosive compound of mercury that he used on people to the iron bars of his cell. The compound melted the bars and he escaped. If his mercury could melt iron bars, imagine the atrocities it wrought on human skin.

Thankfully, Osborn would not escape justice altogether. After fleeing jail, he landed in Kentucky, where he found himself in a fight with a man whom he ended up killing. That Kentucky town hanged Osborn a few days later. The devil himself should fear Osborn, people said, because his medicine was more destructive than the fires of hell.

Mary Jennings would not live to see her sixteenth year, but eight months later, her murderer would not live to torture another innocent soul.

THE SEPTEMBER OF BLOODSHED

"A Horrible Cutting Affair"

Despite the constant reports of violence we are inundated with every day, we live in a low-violence society compared to the 1800s in the Oil Region. In particular, September 1874 saw a rash of violent acts committed in Northwestern Pennsylvania.

On Monday, September 7, 1874, a woman identified only as Mrs. Henderson of Concord Township (located between Corry and Spartansburg) bludgeoned her husband with an axe. Apparently, axe murders were not all that uncommon in the Corry area, since only two years earlier, in 1872, a railroad worker named James Nevins beheaded Hugh Donnelly, a man escorting him to see a doctor in Titusville, while they were boarded in the Corry jailhouse for the night.

Regarding the murder of Mr. Henderson by his wife, the *Titusville Morning Herald* reported, "A horrible cutting affair occurred yesterday near Concord, Erie County. It seems that there lives a little south of Concord a man by the name of John Henderson, who is intemperate, and between him and his wife serious quarrels often occur." Clearly, another theme in these violent events was drink—often the drunkenness of the husband was a factor in either the wife being murdered or committing murder.

The article goes on: "Some time yesterday the neighbors observed the woman leaving the house in a hurry, and supposed, as usual, a family jar had transpired. In the course of an hour, two women passing found Mr. Henderson lying on the ground near the house weltering in his gore, his head dreadfully gashed—the brain protruding, speechless though conscious." The early days of oil probably conjure many images in your mind, but men lying in the street with their brains spilling out is likely not one of them. Northwestern Pennsylvania of the 1800s was a bit ghastlier than we prefer to imagine it.

Later, Mrs. Henderson was caught attempting to flee. She recounted the event to the police as follows: "She says her husband came home and she got him something to eat, that he went and got his razor and then sat down to the table but soon requested her to take the razor and cut his throat. Upon her refusal, he threatened to cut her throat and started for her with an apparent intention of putting his threat in execution. She fled, and just outside the door he overtook her, when she, in self-defense, seized an axe and dealt her husband blows to the head, which felled him to the ground. She stoutly insists that she acted in self-defense."

The *Herald* took the position that Mrs. Henderson was lying and had attacked her husband during one of their perennial fights. The paper said her recounting of the event was riddled with "strong improbabilities."

On Saturday September 19, 1874, John Henderson died. The next day, a jury was called to decide whether Mrs. Henderson should be taken into custody. She was arrested on Monday morning and taken to jail. However, the intrigue did not end there.

The October 3, 1874 edition of the *Herald* reported that Mrs. Henderson died, a scant two weeks after her husband succumbed to his wounds. It gives no context or story regarding her death. The announcement is included in a small section called "Navigating Around the Circle" with a slew of other local updates. Mrs. Henderson was never even given a first name in the papers.

So, was drink to blame? Spousal abuse? Or did Mrs. Henderson just snap and kill her husband? Had she planned it and cooked up a story to (unsuccessfully) cover her tracks? The world will never know. But the "September of Bloodshed" was not over in Northwestern Pennsylvania.

"A Deed of Blood"

On a typical Thursday morning in Venango County on the southern end of Northwestern Pennsylvania, an act of horrific violence was perpetrated by a mother against her children with seemingly no provocation or motivation. The next day, the *Titusville Morning Herald* was emblazoned with the headline

"A Deed of Blood—A Partly Deranged Woman Attempts to Brain Her Daughter with a Hatchet and Not Succeeding Drowns Herself in a Well—A Terrible and Sickening Recital."

Thursday, September 20, 1874, started like any other morning for the Belser family in Rouseville, Pennsylvania. Mr. Belser was away on business, delivering a load of lumber, and Mrs. Belser roused the family to begin their morning routine. Grace Belser was a family woman, raising her children on a farm situated six miles from Oil City and twelve miles from Titusville. About six months earlier, Grace had given birth to her sixth child. Unlike her other pregnancies and birth experiences, the sixth birth had left her in a different mental state, more anxious and fearful of the future and the possibility of poverty than ever before. When her husband left to deliver his lumber, he acknowledged his wife's odd behavior by telling his children to keep a close watch over their mother. That advice unintentionally foreshadowed the nightmare that was in store for the Belser children.

One of the Belsers' teenage daughters helped her mother kindle the fire that Thursday morning. While kindling, Grace asked her daughter to fetch some potatoes from the cupboard for breakfast. As the girl bent down to retrieve the potatoes, she was suddenly struck from behind, shocking her and knocking her down. As she turned to see what had happened, her eyes fell on her mother, standing over her holding the hatchet that had just struck a blow on her head. As the young girl rose to her feet, her mother struck her again, this time breaking her skull and forcing her to the ground. Fortunately, she did not fall unconscious and began to desperately scream for her siblings to come to her aid.

The eldest Belser daughter heard her sister's pained screams and ran into the kitchen, happening upon the violent scene unfolding before her. She immediately confronted her mother and forcefully attempted to get her away from her stricken sister. After grappling for some time, the girl was finally able to wrestle the hatchet away from her mother, although she was later unable to describe to investigators how she accomplished the feat, as her memory had been affected by the intense adrenaline rush of the moment.

As the sister lay injured but conscious in her pooling blood, the older girl fled out of the house, axe in hand to keep the dangerous instrument away from her mother, and began running for help. The *Oil City Derrick* reported that the Belsers' nearest neighbor was 150 rods away, which equates to almost a half mile in distance. Determined to save her siblings, the girl sprinted toward her neighbor's farm and hoped that her mother's rage would not overwhelm her family in the meantime.

As her daughter ran away with the implement of her crime, Grace Belser watched her from the home's threshold. With no tools readily available with which to further act out any gruesome deeds, Grace spotted the home's water well, a deep drop to a shallow watery pool inside. Settling on a new criminal instrument, she seized her youngest son from the house and rushed outside to throw him into the well. In another act of sibling heroism, the ten-year-old Belser boy rushed to his brother's aid and grabbed him away from their mother. The older boy clutched the younger in his arms and ran away from their mother as fast as he could.

Unable to succeed in any of her plans, Grace Belser committed what would be her final act on this earth. In an apparent fit of mental derangement, Grace threw herself into the well, crashing against the bottom and lying in the two feet of water standing there.

In an act that can only be described as pure love from a daughter to a mother, the injured daughter who had been struck with the hatchet stumbled out of the house and found her mother lying at the bottom of the well. With blood flowing from her head and certainly in a dazed and pained state, she called down to her mother and let down the bucket to try to rescue her. Grace, still conscious, reached up and took hold of the bucket. As the daughter began pulling her up from the well, suddenly her mother relaxed and let go, crashing once more with a splash into the hard floor of the well.

As Grace Belser lay at the bottom of the well, the oldest daughter breathlessly arrived back home with the neighbor she alerted to their terrible situation. The neighbor raised Grace out of the well, but by the time she had reached the surface, she had expired. Although some reports say that Grace drowned in the well, others are certain she died as a result of the injuries incurred by her initial fall and exacerbated by her second drop.

Since the danger was now extinguished, people from around the farm began arriving on the scene to witness the destruction wrought and care for the injured daughter. In tending to the girl, doctors told the papers that they believed she would survive. The children were then questioned as to what could have sparked this terrible behavior by their mother, and one reported that while committing these awful deeds she said, "I must hurry and finish this work as my time on earth is short."

It is possible that Grace Belser was suffering a terrible battle with postpartum psychosis. She had a history of being afraid that her family would become destitute and that she and her children would die. A combination of psychological illnesses likely contributed to the horrific acts she committed that Thursday in September, unaware that in reality she was hurting her children instead of saving them from despair.

The Mayo Clinic describes three different conditions that affect many women after childbirth: postpartum baby blues, postpartum depression and postpartum psychosis. Grace Belser was likely suffering from the latter. The symptoms of this condition include mood swings; sleep problems; irritability and anger; feelings of fear, shame and guilt; difficultly thinking clearly; anxiety and panic; thoughts of harming oneself or one's child; confusion; delusions; and paranoia. Many of these symptoms align with how Mrs. Belser was behaving after the birth of her sixth child. Unaware of the existence of such a condition or what to do when it appeared, Grace Belser was doomed to suffer with her postpartum psychosis, just as her family was doomed to the consequences.

Maternal filicide, or the murder of a child by the mother, is not as uncommon as one may believe. Even though we are now almost 150 years separated from the Belser tragedy, there are still more than five hundred filicide arrests per year in the United States. Forensic psychiatry expert Phillip J. Resnick explained that one-third of mothers who kill their children later die by suicide. He wrote that in cases of altruistic filicide, such as with Grace Belser, "filicide is based on a delusional perception that a child is suffering." In her postpartum psychotic state, Belser was likely convinced that her children were in danger of suffering a fate worse than death. Because she was their mother, it was her duty to protect them, even if that protection included death.

"A shocking tragedy was enacted…near this place today, the horrifying details of which are such as to cause the heart to turn sick, and the blood cold with horror in the veins of the listener," reported the *Titusville Morning Herald* on September 21, 1874. In failing in her attempt to kill any of her six children, Grace Belser threw herself into the void, ending what was plaguing her mind and finally putting her at rest. The September of Bloodshed had come to an end, leaving six children battered and motherless and Northwestern Pennsylvania stained with a memory it was eager to forget.

The "Sensation at Corry"

Unfortunately, bloodshed in Northwestern Pennsylvania did not come to an end with the close of the nineteenth century. In 1908, the small Erie

County town of Corry was rocked when the bodies of two well-known locals were found bloodied and in the beginning stages of decomposition by a letter carrier.

At about four o'clock in the afternoon on Saturday, February 8, 1908, a substitute letter carrier lightly pushed open the door to the apartment above the Peerless Theatre on West Main Street to set the residents' letters inside. As the door swung open, his eyes landed on Albert Damon, who was sitting unmoving in his living room chair. Looking at Damon's face, the letter carrier saw blood covering his nose and mouth, dried on his clothing and pooled on the floor. He immediately fled for help and alerted the authorities to the crime scene.

Local police raced to the apartment and were accompanied by Detective Watson from Erie. They immediately found the body of sixty-one-year-old Albert D. Damon, owner and proprietor of the Peerless Theatre above which he lived. After exploring the rest of the apartment, the police also discovered Jane Saterlee, the seventy-one-year-old sister of Damon, lying on the bed in the bedroom with her face, the blankets and the floor covered in blood. The *Titusville Herald* reported, "First evidence was that they had killed themselves and the authorities searched for information concerning a supposed suicide pact. But after the coroner's physician had completed an examination and had found evidences of violence, the theory of murder gained ground rapidly."

The physician determined that brother and sister were killed by a blunt instrument. Damon suffered a mangled and broken nose, broken jaw, fractured shoulder and other bruises. Saterlee's nose was also viciously broken, and her body was covered in bruises. At first, investigators thought the motive was robbery, as Damon was a well-off businessman, but nothing was stolen from the apartment and the dead man's pockets contained a considerable sum of money. Information was quickly ascertained that Damon had recently changed his will, so a possible suspect could be someone affected by the change.

Without making an explicit connection, the police arrested Damon's stepson and closest family member in the region other than his estranged wife, Alice. Twenty-two-year-old John Silloway, the son of Damon's widow to her second husband, was intensely questioned in the town lockup, but the young man refused to talk. Alice had gone to live with her son after fighting with her husband a few weeks earlier. Albert subsequently summoned his sister to help him keep house in Corry while he and his wife were separated.

The town empaneled a jury of six local businessmen to determine the validity of keeping Silloway in jail. Three days later, with Silloway in jail the whole time, the jury charged Silloway with accessory to murder. At the hearing, no media was allowed in, much to the chagrin of the local papers. The jury did not say what his exact role was in the murder, nor did any of the gentlemen illuminate the murder weapon. It was also revealed at this time that Silloway had been kept from his lawyer since being taken into custody, and there was no intention of letting him convene with the lawyer anytime soon. The "most brutal murder in the annals of Erie County" had someone to pin it on, and the public was hungry for justice.

Not everyone was so happy to see Silloway charged. About two weeks after charges were brought, warrants for the arrest of three more men were issued regarding the murders of Albert Damon and Jane Saterlee. Much to the sensation of the town, the names of the accused were familiar: Alpheus

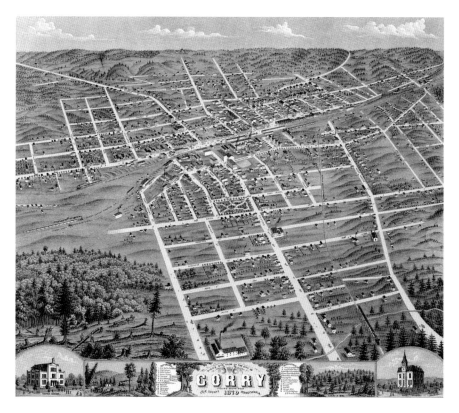

Detailed map of Corry, Pennsylvania. *Ruger & Stoner, 1870.*

Damon, brother of the deceased; Clyde Damon, nephew of the deceased; and Earl Damon, another nephew. Adding insult to injury, the names of the three Damons were given to the police by none other than Alice Damon, widow of the murdered Albert Damon and extended family of those arrested. According to the police, Alpheus was the chief beneficiary of Albert's property, real estate and life insurance policy upon the event of his death and, thus, why Alice suspected him and his familial associates of the murder.

Almost immediately after the warrants were issued, Alpheus was brought into custody, and the two nephews willingly gave themselves up. On Saturday, March 7, 1908, Silloway and the three Damons were all brought before the judge for a hearing as to the propriety of formal charges. Several thousand people from the community clamored to witness the proceedings. Multiple people took the stand and testified that they saw John Silloway leaving the Damon residence on or around the day of the murders. Even young Daisy Bull, only fifteen years old, stood up under intense cross-examination and was staunch in her assessment that it was Silloway she saw exiting the apartment that Saturday afternoon. The judge determined that there was enough evidence to bring formal charges against Silloway, and the young man was led back to his jail cell with a wave and a smile to the large crowd. In contrast, the same judge also decided that there was no evidence against any of the Damons, and they were all freed, to the raucous cheer of the crowd.

Even though someone was formally charged with the murders, the twists and turns of the case were not yet through. On March 17, 1908, LaVerne King and Albert Brennan were arrested in connection to the murders. King and Brennan, the thirty-six-year-old half brother of John Silloway, were held in jail for three days before being released. Less than a week later, Brennan decided to make a public statement regarding his arrest. Brennan stated that he was disgusted by the "bull-dozing" tactics of the police and investigators, that he was wrongfully arrested and that his half-brother, John Silloway, was completely innocent.

On May 13, 1908, John Silloway was indicted by the grand jury in Erie for being an accessory to murder. The *Titusville Herald* reported that the examining physician declared during the grand jury proceedings that an anonymous person offered him $300 (more than $7,500 today) to strengthen his testimony against Silloway. Apparently, the physician refused, but public suspicions were already rising as to the probability of Silloway's guilt. At this point, Silloway had been imprisoned for more than three months, with no set bail or possibility of release before trial. Silloway's lawyer pleaded for his bail to be set, and finally, after almost four months, the judge set the bail amount and Silloway was freed almost instantly in early June.

Silloway's case was put on the fall criminal trial schedule in Erie County. September dawned quickly for the county attorneys, and when the date arrived, they were unprepared to present a strong case against the young man. On September 23, 1908, the county prosecutor announced his intention to drop the charges against Silloway due to lack of evidence. In addition, multiple doctors were prepared to testify on behalf of the defense that Damon and Saterlee were not murdered at all, but rather died by suicide.

In October of that year, the case was briefly argued in front of the judge as to whether a trial should or should not commence. Unfortunately for Silloway and the reputation of criminal justice in Erie County, the judge said that "he could not act in the matter until he had looked the law up a little more," and a decision was reserved until "he has had time to look it up." Judge Walling must have been in want of his legal books, as it took him three months to decide what the law was regarding the fate of John Silloway's trial. On January 26, 1909, the judge decided that Silloway must be freed from all charges because two criminal court terms had passed since his arrest without trial, and it was unjust to string him along forever with no resolution. However, the prosecutor was free to bring charges against him in the future.

Shortly after his release from legal responsibility in the county, John Silloway moved to Portland, Oregon, with his mother, Alice, and his half brother, Albert Brennan. Alice Damon reverted to using the surname Brennan in an apparent and understandable attempt to distance herself from both the Silloway and Damon names. Silloway and the Brennans began to make their lives anew out west, but it would not last long for young John.

On February 3, 1910, just two years after the deaths of his stepfather and aunt in Corry, John Silloway was reported dead at age twenty-four. The newspaper reflected on the origin of his local fame, determining that local authorities "bungled" the case; now with Silloway dead and no evidence remaining, the motives of death would remain unsolved.

Albert Damon and Jane Saterlee were buried at West Spring Creek Cemetery near Corry after their untimely deaths. Little did anyone know at the time that the accused would be laid to rest only two years and more than 2,500 miles away in Oregon. While the deaths of Albert Damon and Jane Saterlee certainly lived up to their label as the "sensation at Corry," it begs the question as to whether this sensation ended with two victims or three.

Chapter 2

Broken Bodies on Steel Tracks

Railroad Disasters in NWPA

The Ashtabula Train Disaster

The night was dark, and the snow fell heavily onto the moving train, slick tracks and quiet woods along the Lake Shore Railroad from Erie, Pennsylvania, to Ashtabula, Ohio. December 29, 1876, was like many other winter nights, until at approximately 8:00 p.m., when everything changed.

You may be familiar with the Great Train Wreck of 1918, the worst rail disaster in American history at 101 lives lost. But have you ever heard of the Ashtabula Disaster of 1876? Until 1918, it held the sad title of most devastating rail accident in American history and, although it is lesser known, claimed almost as many lives.

In the early evening of December 29, a train on the Lake Shore Railway had just made its way out of Erie, Pennsylvania, in one of the worst snowstorms of the year. Witness Reverend Stephen D. Peet wrote, "The night was portentous. All nature conspired to make it prophetic of some direful event. The sympathy of the natural with the historic event was known and felt. Ominous of evil, a furious storm had set in.…The snow had fallen all day long, and was, at the dusk of night, still falling with blinding fury. The powers of nature had seized it again and were hurling it down as if in very vengeance against the abodes of men."

Some travelers were persuaded by their families to stay home that night due to the storm, but others were determined to reach their destinations.

This engraving appeared in *Harper's Weekly* and showed the nation the horrific aftermath of negligence and weather on the railroad. *From* Harper's Weekly, *January 20, 1877.*

As the train surged westward, men, women and children aboard settled in to their nighttime routines. Young professionals sat down to a game of cards, while a few older gentlemen spent time in the smoking car. Some ladies and their children bid one another goodnight in the sleeping car, expecting to be awoken when they reached their destination.

Peet wrote that suddenly

> *the sound of the wheels was stopped; the bell-rope snapped; the lights were extinguished; and in an instant all felt themselves falling, falling, falling. An awful silence seized the passengers; each one sat breathless, bracing and seizing the seats behind or before them. Not a word was spoke; not a sound was heard—nothing except the fearful crash. The silence of the grave had come upon them. It was the fearful feeling of those who were falling into a fathomless abyss. The sensation was indescribable, awful, beyond description. It seemed an age, before they reached the bottom. None could imagine what had happened or what was next to come. All felt as if it was something most dreadful. It was like a leap into the jaws of death, and no one can tell who should escape from the fearful doom.*

The iron bridge was pioneered in 1865 by the president of Lake Shore Railway, Amasa Stone, and passed through regulations (admittedly with deep reservations) by Charles Collins. Based on the Howe truss, the bridge was deemed unsafe by many an engineer and inspector, as the braces were too small and the weight too much for such a structure to handle. After eleven years of bridging the gap over Ashtabula Creek, the bridge collapsed on December 29 under the weight of the snow and the train. The two express cars, two baggage cars, two passenger cars, the smoking car, the drawing-room car and three sleeper cars plunged more than seventy feet into the ravine below.

The crash of the cars killed indiscriminately, and that alone was not the end of the terror. Because the train used lamps and stoves, a fire instantly broke out and spread throughout the cars. As the survivors began to escape, some found that their wounds prohibited them from moving and they were swallowed up by flame. Peet wrote, "Horror seized the living, for death now claimed its victims, and man was powerless to deliver. Within the awful canopy the flames shot up, and from among them came forth groans and shrieks and cries of agony and despair." The wounded were helpless to do anything but watch as men, women and children, trapped by the wreckage, were overcome with heat and flame and cried into the night for help that would never come.

As the flames raged, some of the wounded stepped out onto the ice below the train, which then broke beneath them, the icy waters of Ashtabula Creek pulling them under. The rest of the survivors stumbled onto the snowy shores and waited for rescue, dazed from their trauma.

Soon, people from the nearby town of Ashtabula came upon the scene after hearing a ruckus. The fire department roared to the gulf, but the captain refused to put out the flames, to the horror of the townspeople and victims. Because Ashtabula did not have a hospital, wounded people were taken to private homes for care. Although this was the only way many were able to survive, some victims were also robbed of their valuables, and much plundering of the burning train cars was witnessed.

The extent of the damage was in full view as the sun rose the morning of December 30, 1876. Broken bodies lay strewn across the ravine, smoldering in the last of the flames. Of the 159 people aboard the Lake Shore Railway train, 92 people died either instantly or from their injuries and 64 more people were injured; 48 of those who died were unrecognizable due to the fire.

In February 1877, investigations were completed into the cause of the disaster and the responsibility. Both Amasa Stone and Charles Collins

Postcard of Ashtabula train disaster wreckage, February 12, 1910. *F.M. Kirby Company, Wikimedia Commons.*

testified before a court about the design and construction of the bridge, and Collins admitted that it was structurally deficient. On February 8, 1877, Charles Collins was found dead of a gunshot wound in his home with a revolver in his hand. While society accepted the story of a suicide, police detectives determined that because of the angle of a bullet lodged in the wall beside Collins, his death was actually a homicide. However, they did not investigate his murder, as public sentiment surrounding his death was not much aggrieved. Charles Collins was the last casualty of the Ashtabula Disaster.

At the conclusion of the trial, it was determined that the railroad was indeed responsible for the egregious loss of life. But that meant little to those who lost their family and friends to the railroad that dark and fateful night in 1876.

THE TITUSVILLE SLAUGHTER

Snow and poorly made infrastructure were not the only causes of disaster on Northwestern Pennsylvania railroads. Sometimes, calamities of death and destruction were caused by sordid business practices, human impatience and error, such as in the case of the "Titusville Slaughter" of 1865.

On a warm summer day in August 1865, crowds boarded the Oil Creek Railroad in Corry, Pennsylvania, with the goal of traveling to Titusville, about twenty-four miles southwest in Crawford County. The Oil Region of Northwestern Pennsylvania was progressively growing more interconnected, as oil needed to be shipped out of the valley to markets across the country.

In addition to shipping oil, railroads also carted passengers from boomtown to boomtown. The population of the region was surging by the day, and the newborn infrastructure could barely keep up. Unfortunately for passengers, railroad owners and operators were not interested in making the ride any more comfortable than necessary. Financial prosperity and economic frugality were the top priorities, with successful transport coming second and the safety of human passengers falling last.

On Thursday, August 24, 1865, around noon, the Oil Creek Railroad Express train was arriving in Titusville from Corry, carrying freight and hundreds of people spread across passenger cars, baggage cars and open platforms. As the train rounded a sharp curve coming into the west end of the city, engineers immediately saw their worst nightmare: a freight train was coming at them head-on. In a desperate attempt to save their lives, operators of both trains threw on the brakes and jumped from the cars to safety as the two massive trains collided in a loud crash of metal behind them.

The *Titusville Herald* reported that the train crash resulted in a "perfect demolition of locomotive, tender, express and baggage cars, the instantaneous death of six passengers, and the serious injury of a number of others." Hundreds of people from the surrounding area converged on the scene to lend aid or simply to stand in awe of the terror unfolding before them. Rescuers struggled to cut open the sides of the train cars in order to save those still alive and recover the bodies of the dead. Screaming, crying and frantic shouting filled the air as both onlookers and victims struggled to make sense of what had just befallen them.

As people were pulled from the wreckage, it was immediately evident that the train collision was of an extremely serious nature. The dead included William Baldwin of East Cleveland, Ohio; Fred Jouh of Buffalo, New York; J. Edgar Clough of Corry; and Gideon Lightfall of Belfast, New York. Two more men were soon to join them in death. Alvin Potter, age nineteen from Groveland, New York, was found barely alive. Both of his legs had been severed, and his arm was broken. He quickly expired after being pulled from the train. Another man, who could only be identified as Mr. Sedgwick from

Corry, was severely injured and transported to the Morey House near the passenger station, where he also succumbed. Only hours after the ghastly crash, six lives had been claimed.

In a terribly ironic twist of fate, just prior to the crash, Clough was speaking with an acquaintance on the train about how his parents wanted him to quit working on the railroad because they believed it too dangerous. He did not plan to quit his job and said to the man that he did not fear for his safety. The acquaintance recounted to the *Titusville Herald*, "Scarcely had he concluded the sentence when the fearful collision occurred which instantly hurled him into eternity," confirming his parents' fears.

In addition to the dead, there were many horrific injuries reported by the newspaper. Joseph W. Houghtailing of Lafayette, New York, was listed with severe internal injuries; F.E. Joslyn of Corry suffered a compound right leg fracture, meaning the break was so severe it had pierced through the skin, resulting in the amputation of his leg; Steele Green of Hydetown suffered his right leg amputated; Randolph Phillips of Hastings, New York, saw his left leg amputated; Charles Selky of Buffalo, New York, experienced severe internal injuries; Charles Stock of Buffalo endured injuries that demanded both legs be amputated; George H. Coney suffered body and head contusions; Michael Hennesy of Rochester had an injured shoulder blade; and M.R. Dyer of Corry suffered a contusion of the head and right leg. Since the severity of some of the wounds suffered by the injured was extremely high, it remained to be seen how high the death toll would rise.

While the victims and rescuers were trying to pick up the pieces of the slaughter, others were more interested in seeking revenge. The Oil Creek Railroad (not to be confused with the Oil Creek and Titusville Railroad, or OC&T) was chartered in 1860 and connected to Titusville through the Monroe Street station in 1862. The main line eventually was lengthened to travel thirty-seven miles across Northwestern Pennsylvania, connecting towns from Corry to Petroleum Centre. To ride the length of the train line took two and a half hours. Once the train arrived in Corry, freight and passengers would transfer to either the Atlantic and Great Western Railroad or the Philadelphia and Erie Railroad, which was part of the Pennsylvania Railroad.

By the time the great accident occurred in the summer of 1865, the train had been running to Titusville for three years, and people knew just how difficult it was to get a comfortable ride across the region. The Oil Creek Railroad was infamous for selling more tickets than it had available seats, thus forcing passengers into non-passenger cars or standing on open platforms for the length of the trip. People decried the danger this put travelers in, but the railroad refused to address the problem. After August 24, 1865, it would be forced to reckon with the wrath of the public regarding its track record of maltreatment.

In the *Titusville Morning Herald* the day after the accident, there appeared many letters to the paper's editors advocating for justice. More than a few supported the public institution of mob justice against railroad officials because they believed the law would not hold them accountable. One person, identified only as "VIGILANCE," wrote that the citizens of Titusville must "[t]race the guilt fairly and surely to whom it belongs, and see to it that he is punished to the full extent, and though it would be a very poor use to make of a decent tree, still the murderous wretch would be the better for hanging." He went on to say, "I would have any who are guilty of the frightful slaughter today hanged—yes hanged as high as the tree can be found in our borough, strong enough to bear their miserable carcasses."

The willful negligence of the railroad caused this "most damnable murder," and the president, officials and employees of the railroad saw dollar signs instead of human beings. Since people had no other efficient means of travel between towns, the railroad was their only option, and the Oil Creek Railroad held a monopoly in the region. A local appealed to the emotions of potential riders, saying, "You, too, to-morrow, or next week may be brought home to your wife and children a crushed and lifeless corpse, leaving that wife and children helpless and dependent upon the charities of the world—and what care our Oil Creek Railroad monopoly, so that they only save a dollar?"

Two days after the collision, a coroner's jury was called, and it determined that responsibility for the accident firmly lay on Joseph Funk, the engineer of the freight train, and Patrick Carey, the conductor of the freight train. The investigation showed that when it was learned the express train from Corry was running late, Funk and Carey were too impatient to wait for its arrival before taking out the freight train. The Oil Creek Railroad, given its history of parsimoniousness, had not built multiple lines from which trains could switch and thus not crash. Funk failed to correctly estimate how long he had until the express train reached him, thinking he could switch lines before the trains met. Before reaching that point in the tracks, and failing to send out a flagger who would alert him if there was an oncoming train, Funk's impatience claimed the lives and limbs of many passengers. Knowing that he was responsible for the crash and loss of life, after he jumped from the train to avoid the impact, Funk fled the scene. But he was not the only one to be held responsible.

A few days after the crash, one of the recovering victims took a turn for the worse and died. Steele Green of Hydetown was a well-liked Civil War veteran who returned from the war only to have his leg amputated in a train collision. Upon boarding the train in Corry on August 24, Green specifically asked for a seat and was denied. He continued to search for one, but unable to procure a place to rest, he was forced to take up residence exposed and standing on one of the moving platforms. All of those who perished in the crash were in one of those two locations, and Green was the final member to join the ghoulish club.

After Green's death, a second coroner's jury was called to pin responsibility on the guilty parties. They called for the apprehension and trial of the Oil Creek Railroad president, Thomas Struthers of Warren, as well as directors and managers. The public was extremely pleased with this warrant, finally holding those in charge accountable for the terrible accommodations provided to passengers on their railroad.

At the November 1865 inquest into the death of Steele Green, the Crawford County Court charged Funk, Carey and the administrators of the Oil Creek Railroad with criminal liability. The court noted, "We further find from the evidence, facts, and information which have come before this jury that the equipment of the Oil Creek Railroad, its insufficient passenger accommodation, inability to bring the passenger cars and baggage to a platform, want for facilities for loading or unloading freight, creates unnecessary risk of loss of life and property, all of which evils a reasonable outlay would remedy, and be the not only true economy, but tend to save life and limb, as well as property." Officially, the Oil Creek Railroad was responsible for the lives of its passengers, and if it did not provide adequate protection from loss of life and limb, the culpability would rest on the administrators of the railroad.

In the February 1866 session of the court, Thomas Struthers, Oil Creek Railroad president, was charged with manslaughter in the deaths of Clough, Lightfall and Baldwin. However, the jury declined to indict Struthers on the charge, and the case was dropped. In the same session, Joseph Funk and Patrick Carey were charged with manslaughter in the deaths of Clough, Lightfall and Baldwin, and the jury returned an indictment on February 15, 1866, but no trial records for either defendant have been found.

Just as in the Ashtabula Train Disaster, a decade later, the only court that held anyone truly responsible for deaths on the railroad was the court of public opinion. The industrial monopolies that governed life in nineteenth-century Northwestern Pennsylvania made many a man rich who was privileged enough to stand idly by while the rest died trying.

THE SILVER CREEK DISASTER

One would think that after the disasters in Titusville and Ashtabula, railroad regulations, rules and operation would have improved by 1886. Many residents of Northwestern Pennsylvania excited to experience the natural power of Niagara Falls for the first time that year would become the victims of a transportation system still fatally flawed.

On Tuesday, September 14, 1886, a train departed from Erie, Pennsylvania, on the Nickel Plate Railroad bound for Niagara Falls, New York. The train was loaded with people from Erie and the surrounding regions of rural Erie and Crawford Counties and was filled mostly with working-class men employed by local industries as well as their managers and employers. The train left at eight o'clock in the morning with more than four hundred souls on board. The train stopped at depots in North East, Pennsylvania. and Ripley, Westfield, Dunkirk and Silver Creek, New York, to pick up additional passengers. Unbeknownst to the riders, Silver Creek was the last station they would see while on this earth.

While at the Silver Creek station, the engineer on the Nickel Plate train "received orders to run ahead regardless of local freight No. 6 which the order stated would side track for him below the station." He pulled his train, of now eleven cars loaded to their full capacity, out of the

station. The train proceeded "as far as the sharp curve two miles below the station" when disaster struck. Peering around the curve, the engineer saw wafts of smoke floating over the hilltop in front of him, around which the curve traced. Instantly, he knew the smoke was emanating from an oncoming train, destined to meet his head-on. The engineer immediately began sounding the warning whistles and slammed on the brakes, but it was too late. The freight train speeding toward him was topping forty miles per hour and apparently intending to get on the side track out of the way of the passenger train. Neither train would ever reach the side track.

As the trains sped toward each other, the conductors and engineers on both trains jumped to safety and could do nothing but cower as the horror unfolded before them. In a deafening roar, the freight train and passenger train collided on the track, twisting into a mash of metal, steam and human flesh.

The force of the impact instantly lifted the baggage car from the tracks drove it through the smoking car, tearing apart everything and everyone in its path. The *Erie Morning Dispatch* described the horrific scene: "Starting in at the forward end of the car it literally mowed down the seats and crushed their devoted occupants or ground them into unrecognizable masses on the floor. Out of the thirty-five occupants of that car but two escaped with slight injuries."

The crash occurred in a deep gash of land just where the curve begins to round the hill. Passengers in the rear cars were startled by the unusual motion and loud noises making their way backward from the front of the

Panoramic shot of railroads in downtown Erie, Pennsylvania. *Haines Photo Company, 1912.*

locomotive. The sharp whistle of steam escaping from the train alerted locals that something was amiss, and they came running to the scene. In less than ten minutes, more than five hundred neighbors had raced to the track, only to be greeted by the most horrifying sight their eyes had ever witnessed.

As word began to spread that the Nickel Plate passenger train had crashed with a freight train on its way to Niagara Falls, panic set in among both the loved ones of passengers and railroad officials. Across Erie, neighborhoods were flooded with people coming out of their homes, wandering through the streets and asking their neighbors if they had any news about what happened on the railroad. "The streets were alive with people hurrying hither and thither, some directing their steps toward the railroad depots, others seeking the telegraph offices and the newspaper offices, where the latest bulletins were displayed," wrote the *Erie Morning Dispatch*.

Some railroad executives reacted to news of the disaster appropriately, immediately dispatching special trains from Buffalo and Erie carrying doctors and medical supplies to aid the dying and wounded. Unfortunately, this sympathetic reaction was not the prevailing sentiment at the railroad offices. As soon as word reached some Erie depots, officials quickly left the business and closed the doors. Just a few workers were left to field the flurry of questions descending on them by the bereaved and worried, but they did not seem to harbor much sympathy for their plight. The newspaper reported:

> *At the Nickel Plate depot there was a large crowd in attendance. The waiting rooms were filled with men whose eager faces and quickened breath exhibited their intense anxiety. Women stood around with red eyes and begged for information from the operators within. No attention was paid to their pleadings. All through the long afternoon they hung around but the unfeeling telegraphers declined to give them even one small word of comfort, although they were at their wits end to know what to do, and it was not until toward evening when people came from downtown who had secured the facts and a list of the victims that the griefstricken ones were able to learn anything about what had become of their friends.*

Loved ones' worst fears were confirmed when the first train carrying the injured pulled into the Nickel Plate depot. The throng of onlookers crowded onto the platform, murmuring to one another about what they might see when the train began to unload. As the doors opened and people were being carried out, the crowd crushed in on the train, making it very difficult for the

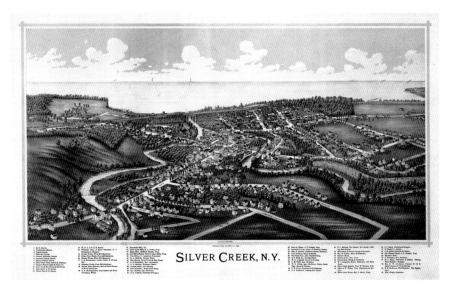

Detailed map of Silver Creek, New York. Notice the Nickel Plate Depot in the upper left corner. *Burleigh Litho, Troy, New York, 1892.*

workers to remove the wounded. As more and more passengers with injuries ranging from minor to grave were unloaded from each succeeding train, the crowd of onlookers became increasingly desperate for news about their individual family members and friends. Little did they know the horrendous scene still unfolding miles away in Silver Creek.

Those who were removed with moderate injuries were from cars farther away from the site of the direct impact. At the collision site, the train cars were still wrapped together with people inside either already dead or dying. The *Erie Morning Dispatch* reported that the site of the wreck was "horrible. The smoker had been bursted [*sic*] by the telescoping, and from the cracks in the corners and seams in the floor oozed blood in streams, making large pools upon the ground." The reporter described how one young man of only eighteen years old was "caught between the telescoping car and the window casing. His body half projected out into the air through the window. His legs were crushed to jelly between the cars, and in his agony he called upon bystanders to put him out of his misery." Moans of the dying and gravely wounded could be heard floating from throughout the smoking car, while locals and fellow wreck victims could do little but stare in shocked paralysis, unable to gain entrance to remove them from the twisted metal.

In a desperate attempt to pry the two trains apart, bystanders cut down a pine tree, stripped it of its limbs and tried to use it as leverage to pull the baggage car off of the smoking car. Despite hundreds of people using all their strength to push and pull against the cars with the trunk of the tree, the smashed metal would not budge. Over the course of two hours, people were able to pull ten victims from the smoking car, without many survivors. After the tenth person had been freed, the wrecking train from Buffalo finally arrived to push the cars off the track and separate them. As the wrecking train began its ghastly work, the scene became horrific once again. The first few pushes by the wrecking train did not work, as "the car after being raised a few inches would fall back and the work of lifting would again be commenced. At such times the strain would open the seams and corners of the smoker and at every turn of the jack, the blood, which was constantly dripping to the ground, would spurt forth in streams." Such a graphic image would only be exacerbated once the cars were finally pried apart and rescuers were finally able to enter the smoking car.

Once in the car, "it was plainly seen how the terrible work had been done. Heads, arms, and legs were lying about, while bodies were horribly mangled, many of them being crushed into a space of a few inches. Brains and blood covered everything. It was literally a death trap from which there was no escape," wrote the reporter from the Erie newspaper. Bodies were carried out to the freight house and laid out in a row. People walked down the line, lifting the coverings on the face of each corpse to see if he was their loved one or friend and "hoping perhaps to recognize some familiar line in those distorted countenances in which they could find a clue to relationship."

Despite the mass of death and destruction, some stories of immense luck and joy emerged from the rubble. One man, Charles McSparren of the Stearns Manufacturing Company, was in the smoking car when the trains collided. He was thrown along the top of the seats and his clothes were torn off before he was thrown out the window by the force of the impact. He suffered only slight bruises, even deciding to promptly continue his journey to Buffalo on another train. Another man in the smoking car, identified as A. Campbell, said that he watched the baggage car go straight over top of him. The car tore off his clothing, but he survived with only cuts and scrapes.

The most miraculous story was told by two men, Mr. William Reifel and Mr. Henry G. Fink, both prominent businessmen of Erie. Reifel and Fink were seated next to each other in the rearmost row of the smoking car on the left side. As the trains hit each other, "They saw the baggage car start and come with terrific force into the smoker. They saw the people in front being literally mowed down, and heard the agonizing cries of the wounded. They witnessed the frantic endeavors of some to escape, but were paralyzed with fright, and sickened beyond description by the horrible sight before them. Had they known that they were to be crushed the next instant, they could not move. Providence however favored them beyond the ordinary among allotted to man. The baggage car, after passing through the car, and killing and horribly mangling nearly all the passengers, stopped a few inches before their faces, and they were saved." Of all the people who were pulled from the train that day, Reifel and Fink, despite being in the car with the most death and agony, were the only ones to escape without any injury at all. The Silver Creek disaster was over, but the effects would be felt for a long time to come.

In the days following, the *Erie Morning Dispatch* printed the names of the dead who could be identified, including W.W. Loomis, a fifty-year-old shipbuilder from Erie; David Sharp and an unknown boy seated next to him; a man named Campbell, who was looking out the window at the time of the impact and decapitated by the oncoming freight train; Charles J. Hersch; John Meyers; M.W. Rastatter; Adriel Heidler; John W. Seifert; Henry Hauk; Stephen Culbertson; W.P. Reynolds; Henry Gebhardt and his son, John F. Gebhardt; J.W. Cudak; Adam Parkhurst; Louis Linse; and two others who were so damaged they could not be identified. Scores of others were injured at various levels of severity, and while some would recover, others later died from their wounds. In total, seventeen people died from the crash and twenty were injured.

A coroner's jury was empaneled to try and assign blame for the horrible event that occurred. Conductor W.H. Harrison and Engineer Lewis Brewer, both of the Nickel Plate train, fled the scene of the crash and did not help any of the wounded or dying. While Harrison was located and questioned, Brewer evaded capture. He was still missing when the *New York Times* reported that he had written to his wife admitting that he made a mistake by listening to the conductor when he signaled him ahead and that he was trying to escape the country. Contrastingly, the *Express* paper in Buffalo reported that Brewer did not run away but was instead seeking medical care for the injuries he sustained when jumping from the train. A few days later, a victim's family reported that a man identifying himself as Brewer showed up to their house to apologize for what had happened. Other victims also came forward and confirmed the story, saying that Brewer had also stopped at their homes to relieve his guilt. Eventually,

Brewer came forward and testified before the coroner's jury on September 22, 1886, but did not accept the blame so easily when questioned.

Ultimately, the coroner's jury could not decide on whom to place the blame. Five jurors said the conductor and engineer were at fault, and four also pinned it on the flagman in his failure to alert the trains of the other oncoming. Whether it was a true accident or a lapse in judgement, a failure to properly do one's job or an impatient railroad staff, the most lasting punishment was once again up to the court of public opinion.

Despite all the death and suffering on the curve at Silver Creek and the cold reaction of the railroad staff to the plight of the families of the victims, there was one bright spot of pure humanity noted by the local news reporter. Back in Erie at the Nickel Plate Depot, Mrs. Sharp, the wife of the departed David Sharp, was sitting in a corner away from the crowd crouched and sobbing with her uncontrollable grief. "No one seemed to think it worthwhile to tender their sympathy to the poor widow," the paper reported. But "by and by a well-known ex hotel keeper chanced to observe her. He approached her kindly, spoke to her comfortingly, called a carriage and procured a supper for her, promising to look after her dead himself." Mrs. Sharp likely had many restless nights ahead, thinking about what was to become of a widow like herself without a husband and possibly heading into the arms of destitution with the railroad so unwilling to help the families of who died in their care. But on some nights, when the din of sorrow quieted around her for a moment, she could take comfort that while death seized lives with equal opportunity, there were still good people in the world—people who on your darkest day would pick you out of a corner, buy you some supper and make sure you were all right.

CHAPTER 3

THE GHOST, THE ASYLUM AND THE INCENDIARY

Unusual Stories of NWPA

SPIRITUALISM: RAPS, GHOSTS AND BOOKS FROM THE BEYOND

Have you ever felt something brush your shoulder and got a chill? Heard a whisper in your ear and been convinced it is the voice of a loved one passed? Wanted to convene with the dead? Well, you certainly would have had a ready-made group of like-minded friends in Northwestern Pennsylvania in the late nineteenth and early twentieth centuries.

In the mid-1800s, a new religious fervor, going by the term "Spiritualism," gained footing in the eastern United States. It is a religion that has now actively existed for more than 150 years. In the United States, it gained popularity in the 1840s when the Fox sisters of Hydesville, New York, claimed to be able to communicate with the dead.

In March 1848, fourteen-year-old Maggie Fox and eleven-year-old Kate Fox said they could hear rapping noises coming from the walls and floors of their farmhouse. The girls claimed that they would ask the invisible presence questions and it would rap on the walls and floors as answers. The children quickly became famous for their spiritual conversations and went on tour demonstrating their powers. Although Maggie later said that she and her sister faked it all, she almost immediately recanted her confession. Unfortunately, Kate died an alcoholic in 1892, and Maggie died in 1893. Despite the demise of its most famous sisters, Spiritualism had already found a strong foothold in American culture.

Photo of woman supposedly taken during a séance—also called a "spirit photo." *S.W. Falllis and John K. Hallowell, 1901.*

The same year Maggie died, the National Spiritualist Association was formed. Spiritualism was not anti-Christian—it actually shared elements of Christian thought, but "unlike their Christian contemporaries, Americans who adopted Spiritualism believed they had a hand in their own salvation, and direct communication with those who had passed offered insight into the ultimate fate of their own souls."

The Victorians were very concerned with death and finding out what might be on the other side, as well as with connecting to their beloved deceased family members. Spiritualism and its elements, such as séances, were an emotional outlet not typically socially acceptable during a period characterized by restraint.

By 1867, Spiritualism was considered a major religion throughout the United States and dovetailed with the growing movement for women's rights. Women were often leaders in the religion and claimed power in a realm where they were often sidelined.

One of the first mentions of Spiritualism in the area was in the late 1870s in Titusville. The Titusville Spiritualist Society hosted parties and dances at the local armory that were well attended and popular. The Titusville Spiritualist Society even claimed the mayor and his wife as some of its most ardent supporters. William and Fidelia Barnsdall, once Methodists, converted to Spiritualism and supported the religion intensely by holding many meetings at their home on North Washington Street. In 1882, their home became the source of controversy when a medium died there.

In the September 26, 1882 *Titusville Herald*, it was reported that Ann Head, a "recluse" from England who lived with the Barnsdalls, died after starving herself. Head "was said to have been possessed of great powers as a medium and endowed with prophetic abilities." She lived in Titusville for at least seven years and rarely entertained company outside the family. She eternally rests alongside her host family at Woodlawn Cemetery.

Titusville was not the only community in Northwestern Pennsylvania where Spiritualism was alive in the nineteenth century. One famous inventor and entrepreneur was a convert and used his inventions to convene with spirits. George Washington Newton Yost was the inventor of the world's second typewriter and pioneer of the American Writing Machine Company in Corry, Pennsylvania. After acting as a consultant on refining the first typewriter—invented by Christopher Sholes, James Densmore (who also had ties to Northwestern Pennsylvania), Carlos Glidden and Samuel Soule—Yost decided that he could improve the machine and sell his own. Yost had previously invented a slew of different machines, including the

Climax mowing machine, the Acme machine, a plough, a traction wheel, a cotton cultivator and a harvester. Although he was predisposed to making and losing fortune after fortune, he continued to throw himself into new ventures. The American Writing Machine Company was his latest venture during his time as a Spiritualist in Corry.

After noticing the shortcomings of the Sholes and Glidden typewriter, Yost decided that his must be capable of producing capital *and* lowercase letters. He also noted that his machine must require simpler upkeep. In 1879, Yost invented the Caligraph typewriter, which fulfilled those necessities, and the next year the American Writing Machine Company in Corry was born. In 1887, Yost improved on this design again and created the Yost typewriter, which had an ink pad in place of the standard ink ribbon and a center guide to improve letter alignment. With his success grew his reputation, which was tied with his Spiritualist faith. It was even said that Yost used his typewriters to convene with the dead, which was confirmed by an explosive book published the year after his death.

Yost died in 1895, and a portion of his obituary was dedicated to his relationship with Spiritualism. The *New York Times* noted, "Although a shrewd man of business, Mr. Yost had a tendency in his nature which led him into abstract speculation and made him a devoted Spiritualist. With a Chicago Spiritualist named Dr. Rogers, he formed a great relationship, believing that the doctor was able to communicate with the spirits of the dead and to record these conversations and interviews upon the typewriter. In spite of the conviction of his friends that Dr. Rogers imposed upon him, Mr. Yost maintained his intimacy with Dr. Rogers in particular and his belief in Spiritualism in general to the last moment of his life." Little could Yost know, but his typewriter would be used for a famous communion with spirits in which he would play a major role, even in death.

Through the typewriter refined and invented in Corry, a man named Joseph Marshall Wade and a medium convened with three spirits in 1896. Wade claimed that spirits told him to get a Yost typewriting machine and place it in a cabinet. He and a medium sat near the cabinet in the dark and watched as the typewriter began to type independent of a user.

Wade claimed that the typist was the spirit of deceased army officer George W. Stevens, supervised by none other than the spirit of George Washington Newton Yost, while transcribing the memoirs of the famous dead medium Helena Petrovna Blavatsky. Wade introduced the posthumous memoir by explaining that it was "dictated from the spirit-world, upon the typewriter, independent of all human contact, under the supervision of G.W.N. Yost,

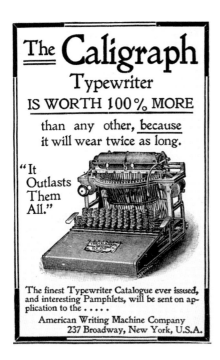

Left: The Caligraph typewriter sold by the American Writing Machine Company, run by George Washington Newton Yost in Corry, Pennsylvania, and used in conversation with the dead. *American Writing Machine Company, 1896.*

Right: A version of the typewriter invented by George Washington Newton Yost, one of his claims to fame. *From* The Yost Typewriter Instructor *by Elias Longley (1891).*

to bring to light the things of truth, and affirm the continuity of life and the eternal activity of the soul immortal."

Wade claimed that the book was a testimony to the truth of the afterlife and the continuation of the spirit and its ability to communicate with the living. He stated that George Washington Newton Yost was the perfect person to oversee this venture, as his "last years of earth life were spent in a consistent endeavor to use the independent dictated writing of his typewriting machine to simplify and lengthen messages from the world of spirit existence." Yost's writing machine was a key tool in the propagation of the Spiritualist faith as it spread from Crawford County, through Erie County and into neighboring Warren County.

West of Corry in Warren, Pennsylvania, Spiritualism was being actively debated in the press. Given Warren's closer geographic proximity to epicenters of Spiritualism, like Lily Dale, New York, it is understandable

Helena Petrovna Blavatsky, London, 1889. *From* Culture and Time, *Wikimedia Commons.*

that the religion often graced the headlines of the local newspapers. In an August 1888 edition of the *Warren Mirror*, a local news correspondent, identified only as "Grapao," traveled to meet a medium and experience Spiritualism for himself with a critical eye. Though neutral in his stance at first, he admitted that "if the claims of the spiritualists are true, there are miracles; and, if those claims are not true, it is a miracle how so many people can be deceived. To the reasonable man it is much easier to believe that spirits return to earth, than to believe that probably one-tenth of all the people in the United States are fools." Feel free to disagree with him, but he had a point in that millions of people were devoted followers of this new religion that claimed communion with the departed.

The Warren reporter wanted to experience his subject firsthand and threw himself into the world of the Spiritualists. He interviewed people who had recently finished sessions with mediums and asked questions regarding how they felt. One woman he spoke with showed him all the evidence accumulated during her session, including slates written on by the dead, and declared that she was completely satisfied with the result provided by her medium.

The reporter even met with a lofty local figure, the Honorable A.B. Richmond, a criminal lawyer from Meadville, who was also there investigating mediums. Richmond acquired the services of a medium and received a message on a slate from C.R. Marsh, a former member of the bar in Crawford County, and was delighted with the session.

After speaking with adherents and witnesses, the reporter finally sat for his own session. He wrote that he was invited to attend a "dark séance, and in company with nine others had some wonderful experiences. Musical instruments floated about in the air, discoursing music of a not very high order. A guitar floated around over the circle, resting now and then upon the head of some person. A small music box also went circling about in the air, and stopped close to the ear of your correspondent, and then nestled under his chin, all the time sending forth sweet sounds." Other items such as watches and pencils floated through the air, taken from people's pockets by the spirits. There were also noises such as raps and bells going off around them. "It seemed as though there were a dozen spirits at work in the darkness," described the correspondent. It occurred to him to ask the spirits to communicate directly with him, and they responded by spelling out the word *Yes*. "If the phenomena were produced by trickery," he wrote, "which does not seem possible, it would be a most remarkable exhibition of dexterity and cleverness on the part of the medium."

A positive opinion of Spiritualism was not shared by all people in the region. The *Warren Ledger* ran a full three-and-a-half-column rebuke of Spiritualism in May 1888 titled "Spiritualism: It Should be Sent Back to Hell, Its Starting Point." This strong language was continued within the article. The writer blamed Spiritualism for taking advantage of people who had fallen on hard times and giving them hope in something false. The writer described how "Spiritualism finds its victims in the troubled, the bankrupt, the sick, the bereft.…It takes advantage of one in a moment of weakness which may come upon us at any time." The writer admitted to understanding how one could be swept up in the fervor of Spiritualism because of how sharp and unbearable the suffering of losing a loved one can be. "If we could marshal a host, and storm the eternal world, and recapture our loved one, the host would soon be marshaled. The house is so lonely. The world is so dark. The separation is so insufferable.…Yes, my friends, Spiritualism comes to those who are in trouble and sweeps them into its delusions."

Warren was not the only community with critics of the religion. In 1896, Spiritualism experienced some religious pushback in Titusville due to the unsavory reputations of some of its leaders dabbling in illegal, or at least inappropriate, business. Followers immediately sprang to its defense. Local leader J. Frank Baxter explained that Spiritualism is a science and "should therefore not be condemned because of the morals of some of its mediums and adherents any more than the science of astronomy should be condemned because of the immoral tendencies of men who were famous astronomers." Even with all its detractors, being a devoted Spiritualist took bravery and strength that many people were still willing to publicly muster.

In Titusville, the Spiritualist Society was not an invisible group in the late 1800s. Many nationally famous speakers graced Titusville with their mediumship, including Elizabeth L. Watson. Watson was originally from the area but had previously moved to San Jose, California, where her Spiritualist beliefs took off. She was the regular pastor at the First Spiritual Union of San Francisco and a speaker at the Golden Gate Religious and Philosophical

Society. Traveling the East Coast on a speaking tour, Watson spoke in Titusville about how Spiritualism for her existed within and around nature. She was an avid supporter of women's rights and suffrage, even serving two years as president of the California Equal Suffrage Association.

In addition to Watson, a husband-and-wife team of mediums came to Titusville in 1897 to give lectures and readings, and in 1900, a séance was held in the parlor of the Hotel Brunswick. Unfortunately, the twentieth century brought the end of earthly life for many early Spiritualists. The next year (1901), former mayor Barnsdall died, and in 1905, oil producer William L. Gage died after serving as president of the Titusville Spiritualist Society for more than three years. His obituary stated that he was educated at the Normal School in Edinboro, worked as a teacher and was a "man of independent thought." Two years later, in 1907, Fidelia Barnsdall also passed away. Despite these many blows, the Spiritualist Society persevered.

Another nationally known speaker, Frank T. Ripley, "celebrated lecturer and medium," visited Titusville in 1914 and gave a speech to the society. Spiritualist member Nellie Lettington was quoted in the *Herald* saying, "It is wonderful to see what Spiritualism has done and is doing to awaken within the thinking man or woman the fact that death has lost its sting and the grave its victory." Many proponents of Spiritualism waxed poetic about their beloved beliefs.

Finally, in 1921, the Titusville Spiritualist Society bought a building specifically for its services. Number 105 North Washington Street became their new home, instead of meeting in members' living rooms and parlors. Its "temple" was completed on December 2, 1921, and was the first place in Titusville dedicated to Spiritualism.

In 1920, Baron Albert Von Schrenck Notzing, a German forensic psychologist, investigated the "phenomena of materialization" and gave credence to followers of Spiritualism. He wrote, "Not only are his powers of observation, his critical judgment and his credibility brought into question, not only is he exposed to ridicule by the reproach of charlatanism…but he even incurs the danger of being regarded as mentally deficient, or even as insane." It was not easy to be a devout Spiritualist in a world seemingly decided against it. Notzing observed medium Eva C. in Paris for four years to try to explore the dark side of "human Soul Life." He concluded that there should be no reason these abnormal phenomena cannot exist, and they most certainly could be tied to humanity. He even went so far as to say that scientifically, the living, breathing individual may only be a "stage in the process of life."

For more than fifty years, Spiritualism held a devoted coterie of followers in Northwestern Pennsylvania. Followers convened with the spirits and one another in their homes and held séances and readings for the public. Although Spiritualism eventually lost its hold in the region, it still thrives in a place not too far from us: Lily Dale, New York. Lily Dale is the modern headquarters of the National Spiritualist Association of Churches and hosts more than twenty thousand visitors every year. Spiritualists may be fewer in number almost one hundred years later, but their legacy and spirit persevere.

KIRKBRIDE'S CURING ARCHITECTURE AT WARREN STATE HOSPITAL

On July 31, 1809, a baby boy was born in our commonwealth who would come to have an immense impact on Northwestern Pennsylvania through his ideas about the mentally ill, asylums and fledgling psychiatry. Almost fifty years before Sigmund Freud was even born, Thomas Story Kirkbride, a Philadelphia Quaker, was educated in New Jersey and became the superintendent of the Pennsylvania Hospital for the Insane.

Before Kirkbride's time, the most common method of treating people with mental illness was to lock them up and throw away the key. Shackles, restraints and tiny damp rooms made up the entirety of life for many patients in insane asylums, what I will term mental hospitals, across the world. Kirkbride had a different idea. Through specialized architecture, light and ventilation, combined with medication and demographic compartmentalization, Kirkbride believed he could not just treat mental illness but cure it.

One of the buildings constructed by the Kirkbride Plan was the State Hospital for the Insane at Warren, now called Warren State Hospital. This institution was the third mental institution approved in the state of Pennsylvania and was established by the legislature on August 14, 1873. The local newspaper, the *Warren Mail*, excitedly proclaimed that the state hospital would be "one of the finest buildings in Western Pennsylvania. Dr. Curwen, who has the main charge of the business, is a quiet, earnest, able, and honest man who understands what is wanted for this purpose perhaps better than any other man in the state." In September 1874, the cornerstone was laid, but the site lay dormant for six years until it was finally dedicated on October 6, 1880, during a large ceremony that included Governor Henry Hoyt and many other state officials.

Warren State Hospital exterior shortly after construction, 1886. *Bairstow, Wikimedia Commons.*

The institution was enormous and beautiful. Constructed from local stone and brick, it measured 1,185 feet and 2 inches long from end to end. Each wing was 40 feet wide, 150 feet long and three stories high. When officials and community members came to christen the building, they were greeted by a long driveway and a tall, spired main hall. The middle of the building contained administration and a concert hall. The *Warren Mail* described how "[t]he windows are large and numerous, and the buildings proportioned so that every part of it is well lighted." It featured iron floor joists, brick arches, floors of Georgia pine and woodwork in cherry, chestnut, ash and black walnut. The institution, unlike other Kirkbride units that only had room for 250, was made to hold 780 patients when full. The newspaper concluded, "Altogether, the institution will be the most perfect of its kind in the world."

And there were many of its kind in the world up to that point. Before 1900, about three hundred Kirkbride asylums were built in the United States. Gorgeously crafted and hulking sites on the landscape, these buildings were not often looked on proudly, but instead seen as "grim reminders of an often inhumane system," writes architectural historian Carla Yanni.

American asylums were constructed in Greek, Medieval and Arts and Crafts styles before the Kirkbride Plan was formulated. Kirkbride combined style with nature, claiming that a positive, naturally pure environment could cure insanity. Asylums were places of immense contradiction, fighting with "tensions between home and institution, benevolence and surveillance, medical progress and social control, nature and culture."

Insanity has always been different from any other kind of health problem. It is the only illness both medical and defined by social norms. In order to know what insanity is, we must know what is sanity. And only the purportedly sane can do that. Over time, insanity has been defined by a range of behaviors including repeated actions, talking to invisible beings and even idleness, poverty and bad luck.

In the nineteenth century, diagnoses of different types of insanity rose dramatically, as did institutionalization of the diagnosed. Physicians believed that the pollution of industrialization and life in cities caused anxiety, stress, depression and other mental illnesses. Those with these disorders could not be cared for by family members who were working full time in dangerous or low-paying jobs. Thus, institutions filled a void of care. In a time when psychiatry was still in its infancy, stately buildings helped legitimize the medical profession.

Families who brought their loved ones to the doors of the asylum were comforted by its quality construction, kind faces and seemingly helpful doctors and nurses. As they retreated from the stone structures without mom or dad in tow, it was easier to assume they were being better cared for in the lush countryside than they would be in the smog-filled cities of home. However, many doctors of the 1800s did not stop to consider that mental illnesses were not just confined to cities. Mental illness did not discriminate between urban and rural dwellers or the rich and the poor anymore then than it does today.

In an attempt to try to address the issue of mental illness for the first time outside the home, psychiatrist Thomas Kirkbride created a design for an asylum, modified by John McArthur Jr., that would give hope to the struggling masses. Unlike other doctors, Kirkbride seemed to understand that mental illness attacked with a ferocity not like any other affliction. In his 1854 book, he wrote, "It is among the most painful features of insanity, that in its treatment, so many are compelled to leave their families; that every comfort and luxury that wealth or the tenderest affection can give, are so frequently of little avail at home; and that as regards a restoration or the means to be employed, those surrounded with every earthly blessing are placed so nearly on a level with the humblest of their fellow beings." Although he says so patronizingly, Kirkbride admitted that mental illness targets everyone, regardless of wealth or familial love.

The Kirkbride Plan gained popularity in the 1840s and continued through the 1880s. It was believed that "the asylum mediates between a person and his or her society. The asylum and its architecture regulated life, limited interaction, controlled activity. It was a place of struggle." Ventilation was considered extremely important to improving the mental and physical health of patients due to the miasma theory of contagion—the belief that human

Corridor of Warren State Hospital, November 19, 1886. *Bairstow, Wikimedia Commons.*

exhalations polluted the air and caused disease. Therefore, a well-ventilated building would reduce disease and its spread.

Kirkbride valued moral treatment of patients, regular schedules, self-control, healthy food, exercise, rural countryside, occupational therapy and a lack of physical restraints on patients. He believed in "early to bed, early to rise" and encouraged institutions to allow patients to stroll about the grounds with the help of an attendant so that they might be exposed to the unpolluted air of rural Pennsylvanian landscapes. While doctors at institutions followed these parameters, they also added treatments via opiates, laxatives, cold baths and more to help "cure" their patients.

The Kirkbride Plan, also called the "linear plan," dictated that hospitals be built in a shallow "V" where each patient room was afforded a view of the gorgeous landscape and promoted natural ventilation. "In most parts of the United States," he wrote in 1854, "during one half the year, there is comfort in the fresh cool breezes that may often be made to pass through the wards, that cannot be too highly estimated, and every precaution should be taken to derive full advantage from them."

He preferred short wards, separation of the sexes and connected pavilions so people could be easily moved from place to place. The superintendent of the hospital lived in the facility with his family in order to create a semblance of domesticity. Wards were used to categorize the sick by their disease so that the most loud and disruptive would be housed farthest from the administration offices and the most docile closest. Kirkbride explained this decision: "The first patients sent to a State hospital are very apt to be of the most noisy, violent, or careless description—those, indeed, who could no longer, without great inconvenience, be kept either at home or in the county jails or alms houses [poor houses]. For these patients, the extreme ranges of the wings are particularly desirable." Wards usually contained patient rooms, a parlor, a dining room, a clothes room, a bathtub room, a water closet, a laundry and rooms for two attendants.

Stone and brick, as used at Warren State Hospital, were the favored materials so that a grand, formal entrance gave feelings of stability, without being extravagant, to family members and friends visiting the institution. "Although it is not desirable to have an elaborate or costly style of architecture, it is nevertheless really important that the building should be in good taste, and that it should impress favorably not only the patients, but their friends and others who may visit it." Therefore, architecture was not only designed for health and well-being but also to calm the fears of friends and family members who were about to commit their loved one to an institution.

In order for the State of Pennsylvania to agree to the construction of an asylum, it had to agree that the chosen site was the correct level of picturesque. In addition, Kirkbride buildings had to be "located in the country, not within less than two miles of a town of considerable size, and they should be easily accessible at all seasons." Warren, Pennsylvania, was immediately agreeable given its proximity to town, hills, valleys and lush Conewango Creek. About 100 acres were required for the building of a new facility, and Warren exceeded this enormously with its original 374 acres directly facing Conewango Creek.

Kirkbride and the state agreed that locations of hospitals for the insane needed to be where patients could exert maximum comfort and happiness. Before construction began, it had to be certified that the land was healthy and fertile, easily tilled and with engaging scenery. Kirkbride wrote that "the surrounding scenery should be of a varied and attractive kind, and the neighborhood should possess numerous objects of an agreeable and interesting character. While the hospital itself should be retired and its privacy fully secured, it is desirable that the views from it should exhibit life in its active forms, and on this account stirring objects at a little distance are desirable." In other words, the landscape should be engaging and interesting, promoting peace and curative well-being. He did not wish for asylums to look like prisons, but instead to have a cheerful appearance.

In December 1880, the first patient was admitted to the State Hospital for the Insane at Warren. The hospital quickly began accepting new patients, but in 1881, it was hit with a tidal wave of about 400 transfers when Danville State Hospital caught fire. By 1896, the hospital was housing 966 patients. In its first sixteen years, it already exceeded its maximum capacity by almost 200 patients.

Dr. John Curwen was the superintendent from the beginning until the early 1900s. The amusement hall for men, Curwen Hall, was named for him, and other structures were built during his tenure such as Eckert Memorial, an amusement hall for women; the greenhouse; a barn; a carriage house; a library; a Turkish bathhouse; and an iron fence around the property. Curwen explained in his 1896 report that the overcrowding was due in large part to the "number of violent, dangerous men, with more or less homicidal inclinations" growing large and "giving rise to constant strife and contention."

The 1896 report shed light on who was being institutionalized at Warren State Hospital and why. Most of the patients were laborers, farmers or wives of laborers and farmers. The numbers of men and women were fairly evenly split. The most common reasons for insanity were attributed to epilepsy, intemperance, "ill health" and "trouble." Other conditions that made the list were masturbation (thirty-seven people), fright (twenty-eight), menopause (twenty-six), disordered menses (twenty-four), domestic trouble (thirty-three), disappointment (thirteen), opium-eating (nine), irregular life (six), religious excitement (five), worry (three), lactation (three), overjoy (two) and nostalgia (one). In addition, fifty-nine women and zero men were diagnosed with "perpetual mania" that year, further exacerbating the harmful stereotype of women as hysterics or intensely emotional people attributable only to their sex.

Of the more than nine hundred patients housed at Warren in 1896, two were under the age of fifteen, nine were under the age of twenty and the majority of patients were young adults or middle-aged, with only one patient over ninety years old. Statistics were highly important in the state hospital system with work, play and medication constantly measured, even to the individual button-holes sewn by women patients in the laundry each year (5,765, if you were wondering). Attendants recorded which arts-and-crafts projects patients were working on and which activities they participated in daily. They documented who constructed the duck pond, picked berries, made bandages, cleaned or worked in the barn, carpentry shop or laundry or on the farm.

Mixed in with those statistics was the number of deaths reported at the hospital. In 1896, 8 percent of patients living at the State Hospital for the Insane at Warren died at the facility. Since its opening sixteen years prior, 832 people had died at the institution. The most common reported cause of death was "exhaustion of chronic mania" or "disease of the brain." In addition, three patients died from strangulation and another seven from suicide. In 1889, one man even died by suicide in a dramatic flourish by slitting his throat with a kitchen knife after finishing his shift in the dining room during breakfast.

While the asylum was a place of refuge for many with serious illnesses who stood no chance of being treated anywhere else, for others it was a difficult, if not impossible, existence. In 1920, the name State Hospital for the Insane at Warren was changed to Warren State Hospital. Kirkbride himself always argued that these institutions should never be called asylums, as that conjured prison-like imagery. The use of "hospital" was appropriate because the mind deserved to be treated just like any other ailment of the body.

Between 1845 and 1910, seventy-three Kirkbride Plan hospitals were constructed in the United States, and five of those were in Pennsylvania: Danville State Hospital, Dixmont State Hospital, Harrisburg State Hospital, Pennsylvania Hospital for the Insane in Philadelphia and Warren State Hospital. Of those, two still exist and are in operation—Warren and Danville, built in 1868 near Bloomsburg.

Warren State Hospital still looks much as it did when built more than 130 years ago. *Courtesy of the author, September 2017.*

The population of Warren State Hospital peaked in 1947 with more than 2,500 patients in residence. Over time, deinstitutionalization has become more popular, and patients stay shorter times before being released. Instead of for a lifetime, the average stay is now around five years. The latest report from Pennsylvania State Hospitals was released in 2014 and stated that approximately 73 percent of people in the state hospital system were there due to schizophrenia and mood disorders. For Warren State Hospital, that number was 80 percent. The population demographics were highest for white, middle-aged men, and most were there due to "extended involuntary commitment" for their own safety or well-being.

Warren State Hospital is a historic institution not just due to its age, but because of its important part in the history of mental healthcare in our nation's history. One of the few remaining Kirkbride hospitals still operates in Northwestern Pennsylvania and employs a great number of people who have dedicated their lives to serving some of the most vulnerable people in our community. Although the history of mental health institutions is not generally happy, Warren State Hospital has become a home away from home for people from Erie, Crawford, Warren, Venango, McKean, Centre and many other counties across the commonwealth. The institution itself is an emblem of a bygone era and a part of the built environment that serves as a reminder of the evolution of mental healthcare in Pennsylvania, the United States and the world.

"CLEAN OUT THE ROUGHS": THE EXPULSION OF STONEHOUSE JACK

Not many people have heard of Robert "Stonehouse Jack" Vance. But in his time, few people were so publicly reviled in the little town of Titusville, Pennsylvania, as the incendiary figure who was threatened with hanging and run out of town.

The first store in Titusville, then a borough, was opened on the southwest corner of Spring and Franklin Streets. A quaint log building, it was home to a dry goods store owned by William Sheffield and opened in 1816. Its first clerk, Joseph L. Chase, eventually became partner and then full owner in 1820. After Chase bought the store, he moved it to the northwest corner of Spring and Franklin, where one of the biggest fires in Titusville history would soon be set.

The sun had set on the night of Sunday, January 22, 1866, but the real excitement was yet to begin. At about 9:30 p.m., the fire alarm rang out, and people rushed to the house of Mrs. Buell on Main Street near Martin, where a blaze greeted them. People formed a bucket brigade to begin putting out the fire to her barn and home while the blaze continued to rage.

Simultaneously, the fire alarm pealed out once again signaling a second fire. Citizens ran to the corner of Franklin and Spring Streets to see the beloved Chase block already up in flames. The Dreyfous and Company liquor store and adjoining E.B. Chase and Company dry goods store were both enveloped in flame, and within five minutes, both buildings were "beyond the hope of preservation." Local firemen of engines no. 1 and 2 desperately tried to extinguish the fire. They were unable to douse the flames due to a sabotaged engine and cut hose.

Some goods were removed from the Chase building, but nothing was recovered from Dreyfous. The losses amounted at over $28,000, not including the total loss of the Chase store. Thankfully, Winson's block and the Titusville Herald Building were saved from the embers. Gazing into the ashes and mourning what once had been was not enough for the people of Titusville. They were ready for revenge.

The *Titusville Herald* explained the factual details of the fire, and the editors advocated for hanging/lynching the culprits to rid the town of undesirable people. The article, titled "The Remedy," reads:

> There are times when the usual machinery of the law for the redress of wrongs, seems to every mind as too slow to meet the demands of the case—times when to do violence to the law seems to be the only sure method of securing the objects for which law is created. This feeling is universal, and those who are usually found cool and calculating, who are the first to counsel against violence of any kind, are often found to be the most positive in the exhibition of this instinctive principle of the human mind.
>
> An occasion of this kind seems to be upon us now. A meeting of citizens is called for this morning at 9 o'clock, to meet at the rooms of the Board of Trade, in Fletcher's Block to inquire into the circumstances attending the fires of last night, and to take such action as the case shall seem to demand. A notorious character, whose name is said to be Robert Vance, but generally known as "Stonewall Jack" [sic], was taken into custody, with three others, whose names are reported as Henry Vanderburgh, George Robertson and Charles McKinney; and if one half the reports concerning them are true, they are most eligible candidates for the halter. Vance, or "Buffalo Jack,"

kept a disreputable house at Shaffer, and is said that he was suspected of causing the late fire at that place. Vanderburg and Robertson, from the "Five Points" of Buffalo, have the reputation of being equal to any such fiendish plot as was evidently attempted last night. McKinney, who kept a gambling house in Pithole, stated, on last Thursday night, that he would bet a thousand dollars that Titusville would be burned down before Sunday night had passed.

There are many rumors afloat, and among them all it is impossible to sift truth from falsehood. Among these reports is one to the effect that two men were taken in the attempt to set fire to the Pomeroy House; that another was seen carrying an armful of shavings under a flight of stairs near Ralph's store on Franklin Street near Spring; and that some balls of rags saturated with some combustible matter and ignited, were thrown into the house of Mr. Moore, near the Bliss Opera House.

A crowd of citizens assembled around the lock-up and would have taken out the prisoners and hanged them if they had not been prevented by the police. This morning let the subject be approached with calmness, but with determination.

It is for the citizens at this meeting to adopt such measures as shall secure an immediate trial of these and others who may be implicated; and if the question of guilt is clear, to see that they pay the penalty of their deeds with their lives. Self-preservation requires it, and the public safety demands it.

Titusville has suffered enough from incendiaries. The town is full of vagrants, harlots, and pimps. Let them be cleaned out en masse. The suspicious characters arrested last night should be the first dealt with. If shown that they had any complicity with these acts of incendiarism, they should be hanged. We shall have no more incendiary fires after one or two desperate characters have been lynched.

The main arson suspect was Robert Vance, also known as Stonehouse Jack, a local boxer (who was known to have lost to the infamous Ben Hogan of Pithole) and ruffian from the Shaffer Farm area of the Oil Region. Still a young man, Stonehouse Jack, who originally hailed from Buffalo, was described as twenty to twenty-two years old with rich mahogany hair, gray eyes, a light complexion and a prominent face, "while the forehead retires precipitately, and the head tapers off at the crown like a cocoanut."

Along with Stonehouse Jack, many other men and women were rounded up and hauled into the board of trade offices across the street from the leveled Chase building to be "tried" for their crimes. The *Titusville Herald* insinuated that most everyone in town approved of executing anyone found guilty of arson or complicity—a scary situation. It was revealed that during the two major fires, fires were attempted at other locations and were thwarted or quickly extinguished. The *Herald* explained that the men in charge of trial and punishment were "the substantial men of Titusville—men whose characters, public and private, is sufficient guarantee that whatever severity they may recommend is imperatively demanded for the public good." Furthermore, one hundred men were selected to round up "thieves, incendiaries, pimps, and harlots," and thirty men composed the Vigilance Committee that tried the "prisoners."

It was decided at the committee meeting that the bad men were supported by loose women—all must go. Groups of people were appointed to patrol the streets searching for suspicious characters. The committee declared that an example should be made of one of these people "as a standing menace to all disreputable characters who approach Titusville in the future." During the melee, a gallows was erected on the ashes of the former Chase building. The almost poetically written *Titusville Herald* article describing the gallows reads:

> As we were busily engaged yesterday afternoon in writing up the incidents of the morning, our attention was called to what appeared to be some preparation for raising a framework on the lot where Chase's Block stood less than twenty-four hours ago. The scene was directly in front of our sanctum windows, and when the frame was elevated to an upright position above the heads of the crowd, it took the form of a gibbet.
>
> This appeared like work, and if the unfortunate men undergoing examination in the rooms of the Vigilance Committee directly opposite, could have looked out upon the scene, it must have suggested to them they might not be long for this life.
>
> We must confess that as the grim figure met our sight it produced a feeling of sickening horror, and we involuntarily asked ourselves if the matter might not be carried too far; but another view of the smoking ruins, the memory of the narrow escape of innocent ones from a horrible death by fire, and the thought that this was a deliberately conceived and cunningly executed plot for a wholesale conflagration, was sufficient to neutralize any feelings of pity for the wretches who set the fires, or to satisfy any doubts about the justice or propriety of the public taking this short road to a redress of grievances. Nay, even these measures do not rest merely upon justice and propriety, but are rendered imperative by virtue of necessity which knows no law.

There seemed to be an especial fitness in the place chosen for the execution, if there was to be, on the ground where the crime was committed; that the incendiaries might have before them, as their last view of earth, the black and smouldering evidences of their blacker guilt. There was no enthusiasm or excitement manifested by the crowd—it seemed to be a matter of business, a case of clear necessity, for which the mind has been prepared by due deliberation and from which there seemed to be no mode of escape which would not involve peril to the dearest interests of society.

This line drawing by Pearson Scott Foresman is an example of the construction of a gallows. *Pearson Scott Foresman, Wikimedia Commons.*

If these things are allowed to go on as heretofore, we know not how many lives of innocent ones— perhaps of women and children, perhaps of the most indispensable members of society—may be sacrificed for no other purpose than to continue for a while longer the existence of those whose crimes have made them a curse to society and to themselves.

We speak thus confidently because we are sure that somebody is guilty of a most horrible crime which calls for the utmost penalty of the law; of the guilt or innocence, however, of the parties under examination we cannot speak as yet, for the Vigilance Committee have not yet concluded their investigations—they will no doubt see that justice is properly meted out.

In the short course of a single day, the investigation was completed, and punishment decided for all people who were seen as undesirable in the city.

The local headline in the January 24, 1866 *Titusville Herald* read, "Disreputables Smoked Out—Wholesale Expulsion of Pimps, Harlots, and Blacklegs—A Thorough Moral Purgation." The article explained that the previous day at noon, the people still in custody were sentenced to expulsion from the city and taken to the train depot, accompanied by several hundred citizens. Stonehouse Jack and his crew—including George Robinson, Henry Vanderberg, William P. Ogden, James Mehanny and Charles McKinney—were all sentenced to expulsion.

The *Herald* explained, "According to their own admissions, they were professional gamblers, and no doubt rightly deserved the halter; but they were guiltless of the specific charge of incendiarism, and we commend the moderation of the Committee in simply banishing them from our midst. That they were duly penitent for their misdeeds, and thankful for their escape from the wrath of an outraged public, was sufficiently testified by their behavior, and if their declarations are of any value they will never trust their precious carcasses within the limits of the oil region again!" It was also determined that the fires were set by piling wood shavings under a stairway or house and set aflame with rags soaked in combustible liquid.

In addition to the suspected arsonists, the committee also sent away the "bullies and bruisers." Excitedly, the *Herald* reported, "Everybody will rejoice at the determination of the Committee to make a thorough and effectual sweep of the entire gang. In our judgment there is no viler wretch in creation than he who, wearing the image of a man, becomes the stipendiary of a prostitute. Clean them out."

The committee also made an official report that was printed in the paper. Committee members admitted that "from the nature of the evidence elicited upon these examinations, the Committee would have been unwarranted in holding these parties accountable for those fires." However, since it was determined they were of "bad character" and "were inimical to the safety and welfare of the community," they were expelled.

Since Robert Vance was a self-admitted gambler and pimp, he was put on the 1:40 p.m. train out of Titusville and sent on his way to Buffalo. He was warned that if he ever returned, a severe penalty would be imposed—death. Although Pithole expected many of these expelled figures to land there and warned that their "police force [was] fully prepared to give them a warm reception," it does not seem that many veered from the trail back to Buffalo, New York.

The next day, January 25, 1866, there was another attempt to burn Titusville. This time, the Corinthian Hall, attached to the *Titusville Herald's* offices, was attempted to be set on fire. Fortunately, it burned out before majorly catching. In response, the city passed an "Ordinance of Expulsion" whereby the police could bring any suspect of ill-behavior in front of the justice of the peace who could then order them expelled from Titusville.

The local expelled ruffians made it to Corry, where they were met by friends who were on their way to Titusville to exact revenge. The *Herald* wrote, "We presume there will be a great display of bonfires and pyrotechnics at the Buffalo 'Points' in commemoration of the safe return of the distinguished representatives." The *Titusville Herald* was clearly proficient in heavy sarcasm. It continued, "When the express train on the O.C.R.R. [Oil Creek Railroad] reached Corry with its precious burthen, a gang of twenty Buffalo roughs were found to have arrived there on their way to Titusville. They were coming here to rescue Stonehouse Jack and his companions or revenge their deaths. One of the men (a brother of Vanderburg, we believe), had bought a coffin in which to carry back the remains of the latter. There was said to have been great rejoicing over the remains."

Despite the threats to his life, Stonehouse Jack was insistent he have the last word. In the January 26, 1866 *Herald*, a letter from him was printed addressed to the citizens of Titusville. It thanked the people for sending him to Buffalo for free and the kind people who accompanied him to the train station. The letter is either a master class in sarcasm from Stonehouse Jack in response to the heavy sarcasm employed by the *Herald* on numerous previous occasions or was sent by a local person mocking Stonehouse Jack. People rightly questioned the letter's authenticity, but the editors said it came in the mail and they knew nothing further regarding its provenance.

Although Stonehouse Jack was threatened on penalty of death to never return to Titusville, he did not completely disappear from local news. On March 14, 1866, a letter from Stonehouse Jack was printed in the *Pithole Daily Record* in response to something the paper printed about him previously. He stated that he was willing to fight Hogan again, and he clarified that he did not have a wife, likely because of his reputation.

The last time Stonehouse Jack was mentioned in local papers was August 8, 1866. It was reported that he was accused of robbery in Canada and that he would likely be extradited by New York soon to stand trial for his crime.

The drama surrounding the 1866 Titusville arsons occurred just before Titusville became a city in February 1866. Titusville was marked by a "large floating population" and was plagued by a high level of vice. In his 1899 book *Our County and Its People*, Samuel Bates wrote, "One 'Stonehouse Jack' was regarded as a desperate character. Whether he deserved all that was suspected of him, it has not been since shown." Although it is impossible to know for sure whether Stonehouse Jack and his compatriots were the culprits of the devastating fires, it is certain that this event led to arguably the greatest forcible expulsion of people from the Oil Region in its history.

The destroyed buildings were rebuilt in 1877 and named the Chase-Stewart block. It was redesigned by famous local photographer John Mather. The building boasted a telephone inspected by Thomas Watson, assistant to Alexander Graham Bell. In 1954, it was separated into three buildings: Cohen's, Thompson's and Bryan's. The upper floor was home to Joseph Pew (Sun Oil Company, later Sunoco), Mather and Joseph Seep. In March 2015, the block was engulfed in flames once again, but survived and thrived, an architectural phoenix.

Thankfully, the Titusville community did not publicly execute Stonehouse Jack and his crew for their alleged crimes and thus be forced to wear that stain on their history. The incident certainly goes to show the might of the region's townspeople when their institutions, citizens and livelihoods are threatened by those bent on destruction. Northwestern Pennsylvanians always stand strong.

Chapter 4

Work, Play, Politics
and Worship in Rural NWPA

Cyclops & Cytemp Steel

Imagine the sound of a strong steel hammer ringing out across town. Couple that with the *clanks* and *clangs* of the presses and the scrape of the cold chisel against solid metal. Visualize the plumes of steam and smoke rising into the sky over a small town booming with activity and surrounded by wooded hills. Here sets the scene for the story of one of Northwestern Pennsylvania's most lucrative non-oil industries: steelmaking.

Steel companies can trace their history deep into our collective past in Northwestern Pennsylvania. In large part, the establishment of steel in Titusville began with Charles Burgess.

Burgess was born in England in 1841 and dropped out of school at the tender age of nine to begin working. He apprenticed in steelmaking as a young man and eventually immigrated to the United States in 1866. Although Burgess would travel back and forth to England many times throughout his young life, he finally settled with his wife and family in Titusville in the 1880s.

Burgess purchased the failing Eames Petroleum Iron Works and converted it into what became Cyclops Steel Company in 1884. With his secret formula, Burgess invented the first high-speed, self-hardening steel tools in America. He was an artist, scientist and engineer all in one. The commemorative fifty-year booklet for Cyclops Steel described Burgess as a master craftsman of his medium. It states that those whom he trained "exhibit a love for thoroughness and for finished work, accompanied by that pride in execution which is characteristic of the artistic instinct." That level of quality in steelmaking was a valued part of his company's reputation throughout its history.

At Cyclops, steelmaking was an art. "There is romance in the manufacture of steel as there is in every line of endeavor originated and propelled by men of vision, action and determination," the company wrote in 1934. While steelmaking was certainly an art, it was also incredibly dangerous. In the early years of the company, there were multiple reported injuries. In 1900, a man named William Joyce had his hands mangled by a hammer. Then, in 1905, a seventeen-year-old worker named John Hartwell was permanently blinded in one eye by a flying metal fragment from a cold chisel. Danger and art walked hand in hand in the Oil Region.

Despite the danger, steelmaking provided a good, steady job. At this time, those who worked in the steel plant labored for nine-hour days making 12.5 cents per hour for unskilled work and 15 cents per hour for skilled work.

As Burgess neared retirement, he sought out investors who could expand the company. In February 1916, Burgess sold the company to Carl Boker & Sons of New York. Still operating under the name Cyclops, the new owners built larger facilities, furnaces and mills. The company also grew as it acquired government defense contracts in making materiel, such as shells and airplane motors, for World War I. Burgess died in 1919, his death marking the end of the first stage of Cyclops's development and the beginning of a new era.

In the postwar years, Cyclops went through hard times financially and needed a change of direction. In 1926, the company hired metallurgist Charles T. Evans to develop new specialty steels. Evans became a driving force in the success of the company over the coming decades.

Evans was the inventor of Cyclops's two most important steels: No. 17 and K Steel. No. 17 Steel was used in seamless periscopes and oil industry tools. It was resistant to corrosion and fatigue. This steel was used by the U.S. Navy in its submarine periscopes and provided a long-lasting contract for the company. K Steel was primarily used in pitch propellers, air navigation, fast transport and diesel engines. Cyclops sold these steels across the country with the company assurance of quality personal workmanship.

In 1935, Cyclops expanded by buying out the American Radiator Company in Titusville. The next year, it merged with Universal Rolling Mill Company out of Bridgeville, Pennsylvania, and changed its name to Universal-Cyclops Steel Corporation.

Cyclops again contracted with the government during the Second World War, and homes were created on Sunset Heights to house the influx of defense workers. Housing there is still used today. During World War II, Cyclops used the former Radiator Company site to produce items for ship turbines and airplane engines. This production continued during the Korean War in the 1950s. Throughout this period and into the next, heavy-duty steam-powered steel hammers could be heard echoing through the valley up to five miles away. Steelmaking became life in the oil valley.

After Evans's death in 1949, Cyclops continued to operate at full capacity, supplying specialty steels to industries throughout the United States and abroad. In 1971, sales were over $300 million and continued to rise.

A large change to the organizational structure came in October 1984 when the company decided that Titusville would be the new headquarters for the Cytemp Specialty Steel division. At that time, the Cyclops name was discontinued, and Cytemp was born. Throughout the 1980s, under the direction of President John E. Buser, Cytemp was successful in producing high-temperature alloys in bar, billet, sheet and strip forms, as well as stainless and high-speed steels in bar and billet forms.

The company hit hard times in the late 1980s, and Armco Inc. was supposed to buy it out in 1991. In April 1992, the companies finally did combine, albeit somewhat unsuccessfully. As a solution, former Armco managers formed their own company, Universal Stainless & Alloy, and in 1994 took over the Titusville and Bridgeville facilities. They remain operating as Universal Stainless & Alloy still today.

The history of Cyclops and Cytemp in the Oil Region is integral to the collective past and memory of Northwestern Pennsylvania. A great number of people across the region can name a family member or friend who worked at least one of the two operations or grew up during the heyday of steelmaking and its economic impact on the region. Cyclops & Cytemp hosted company picnics, sponsored sports teams and even had a founder's club of employees who had dedicated at least thirty-five years of their lives to the steel industry. Steel, like oil, was a hallmark industry of the region and provided livelihoods for hardworking people throughout multiple counties.

The legacy of Burgess, Evans and steelmaking live on. Burgess's daughter, Helen Burgess Doty, gave the land that countless people have since enjoyed and which is named for her father: Burgess Park. The *Specialty Steelmaker* statue that sits on the front lawn of Burgess Park was modeled after Cyclops hammersmith Frank Clark, who dedicated more than fifty years of his life to steel.

Steeltowns today might be smaller, and residents may no longer hear the clang of hammers nor the screech of the barker or the hammering of the oil drill, but the legacy of these industries is deeply imbedded in the hardworking culture of Northwestern Pennsylvania. Just slightly north of those clanging hammers sat an industry that mixed the sweat of hard work with the reward of creating something meant not for war, but for whimsy.

BROOKLYN MEETS ERIE:
MARX TOYS AND INVENTING PLAY IN NWPA

Kids growing up anywhere in the world, regardless of class or status, have one major thing in common: they play with toys. Whether they buy them, are gifted them or create them on their own, toys are a staple of childhood. In the twentieth century, many of the toys most affordable for families with children could be traced to Erie County, Pennsylvania.

Northwestern Pennsylvania has always been full of hardy workers who sacrificed their minds and bodies daily in support of demanding industries. The diversity of industry in this small corner of the state is wide, even lending itself to play. When one thinks of work and play all in one place, many residents conjure an image of a company that formed more than one hundred years ago and employed generations of people in Erie County: Marx Toys.

Although it was certainly hard work for the factory employees, artists, managers and others at the company, the Marx family prided themselves on the creation and manufacture of instruments of play. A "tin toy dynasty," Marx Toys supplied children the world over with affordable toys that inspired countless hours of play, many of which were invented and created right in our own backyard. With locations in Erie and Girard, Marx made itself a home in Northwestern Pennsylvania and heavily affected the region for more than fifty years.

The man who would bring his hallmark toy company to the region was Louis Marx, born hundreds of miles away in Brooklyn, New York, in 1896. By the age of twenty, Marx had climbed the ranks of the Strauss Toys company in New Jersey and attained the rank of manager. He then went to Europe while serving in World War I. After the war, Marx noticed that German toy manufacturers could no longer compete in the American market. Seeing an opening for a booming business in which they could be extremely commercially successful, Louis teamed up with his brother, David, and founded their own toy company, which they called Louis Marx & Company. They incorporated the company in 1919 and opened their first manufacturing facilities in 1921.

Marx first made its mark on the toy business by predicting which other companies' toys would become hits on the market and creating an alternate version that was cheaper to manufacture. At first, instead of using its limited resources to invent and manufacture original toys, it simply remodeled the ideas of others, refined them and profited. The most famous example of this method is its co-option of the yo-yo. In the 1920s, the Marxes found they could make the yo-yo much cheaper than other toy companies and were able to sell around 100 million of the simple toy on a string.

Eventually, the company expanded its production, began creating its own proprietary toys and opened new facilities at Glendale, West Virginia, in 1931; Erie, Pennsylvania, in 1933; and Girard, Pennsylvania, in 1934. Unlike most companies in this era, Marx Toys grew during the Great Depression while many others faded or went out of business entirely. Through their shrewd business tactics, the Marx brothers were able to infuse the areas where they opened up shops with cash flow during a critical period of widespread economic hardship.

Girard plant worker Raymond Hubiak, one of few who had the chance to meet Louis Marx, said that he was always impressed with Marx for having the courage to continue growing and inventing even in the throes of the Depression. Not only did he continue to create, but Louis also provided essential employment for hundreds of families in a time when they could have easily been under immense duress, like most blue-collar workers in the United States. "We all appreciated it very much," Hubiak said. "Jobs were hard to come by," and Marx provided them by the dozens. In short, the Marx company saved innumerable local families from poverty with their choice to open two plants in Erie County in the 1930s.

The Marx brothers, not wholly unlike the comedy family with whom they shared a name, liked to keep things flashy, fun and exciting, all while appealing to the average family. By sticking with the slogan "Mechanical toys that are durable and mechanically perfect," the company gained a reputation as a maker of quality products. By the age of twenty-six, Louis Marx was already a self-made millionaire.

Once in Erie County, the Marx company production and invention soared even higher. The company prided itself on eye-catchingly colorful toys made of tin with lithographs or expertly crafted plastic. Marx expert Maxine Pinsky

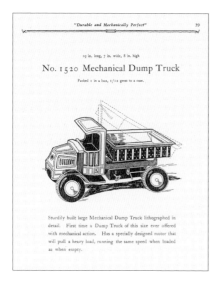

"Durable and Mechanically Perfect" 39

19 in. long, 7 in. wide, 8 in. high

No. 1520 Mechanical Dump Truck

Packed 1 in a box, 1/12 gross to a case.

Sturdily built large Mechanical Dump Truck lithographed in detail. First time a Dump Truck of this size ever offered with mechanical action. Has a specially designed motor that will pull a heavy load, running the same speed when loaded as when empty.

Mechanical Dump Truck by Marx Toys, sold in the 1930s. *From* Marx Mechanical Toys Catalog, *Louis Marx & Company, 1930, page 39.*

noted that at the company, "The range of subject matter covered is staggering, from the realistic to the fantastic, but generally, Marx felt that children liked toys which reflected what was familiar to them." Therefore, they made many trucks, ships, mementos and toys with pop culture references. The main goal was for the toys to be exciting, humorous and moderately priced so that the average family could enjoy all the happiness Marx Toys had to offer.

From its entry into Erie in the early 1930s, Marx was the largest toy company in the world until 1960. It was sometimes colloquially referred to as the "monkey works" due to one of its most successful toys, the climbing monkey, that was used as the basis for many other climbing-based moving toys. Marx capitalized on his success by forging the company ahead into mass production. The "Henry Ford of toys," as he was called, introduced high-volume production into the main Marx plants, cranking out thousands of high-quality, low-cost toys.

Not only did Marx toys stand out because of their cost, but their artwork was also dazzling. With beautiful color, interesting motions and a wide variety of interests, Marx toys were simply some of the most appealing on the market. These toys were meant to be used and played with, as well as appreciated for their beauty. Locals described how playing with the toys showed a "great amount of kinetic energy…and drama," just what children wanted to find wrapped up for their birthday or under the Christmas tree.

Few people in the Erie or Girard plant ever met Louis or David Marx, but those who did certainly remembered the encounter. Ed Furie, David Marx's assistant, described the eccentric man: "You never argued with David Marx. You never said 'but' and if you were right, you were still wrong, and when you were wrong, you were wrong. But then he would bring you back into his office, put his arms around you and say, 'Eddie, why do you make me yell at you? Here's a hundred, buy yourself something.' But everyone knew you were going to get a gift: twenty, fifty, whatever. You see, he always put his hand in his pocket and whatever he pulled out, he'd give it to you.'" One would imagine that after enduring that mental abuse, those who came away with $100 might be more placated than those on the unfortunate end of Marx's eccentricity on a small bill day.

Unlike other toy companies, Marx was extremely slow to begin advertising on television. Executives were averse to the idea, even when other companies such as Fisher-Price and Mattel were increasing their name recognition and stock by beaming directly into families' homes via their televisions. After Mattel saw overwhelming success through television advertising in 1959, Marx executives could no longer deny the tube's influence. Beginning that year, Marx cranked out countless commercials. It even began licensing deals for toys in conjunction with comics, television shows, movies and promotional toys. Commercial advertising was a resounding success for Marx and the toy industry.

Marx artists were given huge creative latitude to try to create the next big thing. Artists at the Erie plant would design new toy concepts, packaging, art, labels and games. Roy Ahlgren, an artist who started with Marx in 1954, said that although one was never assured their work would be produced, many of his designs were. A good number of the Marx products were invented in Erie. Artists there produced layouts, created camera-ready art, wrote copy and built demos and displays, among their other creative duties. Ahlgren noted, "Many times I had to airbrush certain toys or hand-paint samples for the New York showroom. This meant that we had to paint a dozen or so card and box samples for the New York showroom where buyers would decide and put in orders which determined the runs on the assembly lines in the Erie plant." In other words, the work of these local artists often directly determined what was and was not made by the company nationwide.

Secrecy was paramount in art and development, and the Erie plant is credited with creating the box arts for the Big Job Truck, Stutz Bearcat, Mystery Space Ship, Big Loo, Electric Pinball, Hi-Light Scoop & Dump Truck, Apollo Moon Bagatelle and Daniel Boone booklet, among others.

In addition to these classic toys designed in Erie, one of the first train sets affordable for the average family was made in Girard in conjunction with the former Girard Model Works. Toys featuring conflict, war, soldiers, cowboys, vikings, knights and pop culture icons were all commercial successes and manufactured at the Erie County plants. Marx Toys was especially inventive because the company was able to reuse the bodies from outdated toys by combining them with the newest heads and faces

1930 Marx Mechanical Toys catalogue featuring the signature Marx stamp near the top. *Louis Marx & Company, Wikimedia Commons.*

to maximize profit. The consistent goal of the company was to always make toys that lasted and were affordable for everyone. Every child deserved a toy.

One of Marx's biggest commercial successes was fashioned by a creative employee at the Erie plant: the Big Wheel. In Erie, toymakers, including Erie plant manager Raymond Lohr, invented the concept and signature pedal crank, which is now used in toys the world over. The Big Wheel became one of the best-selling and most popular toys of all time; the Marx company alone manufactured 7 million units. The toy is still produced today and has even been enshrined in the National Toy Hall of Fame.

After more than fifty years of continued success, Marx Toys was sold to Quaker Oats in 1972 for $51.3 million. This set off an unfortunate chain reaction of profit nosedives and plant closures. The Erie plant closed in 1975, eliminating the livelihoods of 440 people. The next year, Quaker Oats sold Marx to Dunbee-Combex-Marx for only $15 million. Four years later, in January 1980, the Girard plant was closed, eliminating another slew of jobs in Erie County. Louis Marx died soon after in 1982. Many former employees went on to form their own businesses or became executives in rival toy companies.

Happily, after years of dormancy, American Plastic Equipment Inc. of Miami, Florida, purchased Marx equipment and molds and began manufacturing Marx toys again in 1991. Despite the resurgence of manufacturing, Marx's time in Erie was never to resume. Marx Toys, once the affordable family toy, now draw high prices at auctions, shows and antique sales. These shiny, colorful tin and plastic toys with wind-up and friction motors provided innumerable hours of creativity and play for thousands of children across the United States and abroad. Although Marx Toys are now a relic of the past, this creator of Rock 'Em Sock 'Em Robots, the Big Wheel, beautiful train sets and hardy cowboys affected not only the lives of children but also those in the Erie and Girard communities who survived thanks to the whimsy and business savvy of a few Brooklyn toymakers who took a chance on Northwestern Pennsylvania.

SOCIALISM UNLEASHED AT CONNEAUT LAKE PARK

Growing up in rural Pennsylvania in any decade has been fraught with cries from residents of all ages that there is nothing to do. While that is certainly not true today, it was similarly untrue even before the turn of the century. There were no cars or well-maintained roads in rural Northwestern Pennsylvania. In our corner of Penn's Woods, we happened to boast one thing that the rest of the state did not have: the largest natural lake.

At 497 feet above the surface of Lake Erie sat a lake called "Konneyaut," or "Snow Place." Native Americans were the first inhabitants of the region and enjoyed the three-and-a-half-mile-long and one-mile-wide lake that was "spring fed, producing clean waters and a keenly blue surface." Even before the Native Americans, the area was populated by early mammals such as the mastodon, whose skeletal deposits have been uncovered in the lake's bed.

The first European settler to arrive in the area near the lake was Abner Evans, and the land became known as Evansburg until September 1892, when it was renamed after its most famous feature, Conneaut Lake. As more people filtered into the area to make their new homes, it was discovered that Conneaut Lake was a prime location for the ice industry in the winter and leisurely recreation in the summer.

Canals and railroads were the only modes of transportation in and out of the Conneaut Lake area, and the railroad industry capitalized on the recreational opportunity presented by the lake. Railroad titans knew that there "is a fundamental and gripping magnetism for the human race wherever water meets land," and thus they created tracks leading to this relaxing escape from the "noise, dirt, congestion, dehumanization, and stress" of Erie, Pittsburgh and other large metropolises. Railroads were bringing the people to Conneaut Lake, and year-round residents were preparing to capitalize on the imported tourists.

On April 25, 1892, Colonel Frank Mantor and a group of fellow capitalists formed the Conneaut Lake Exposition Company with the goal of building a park where residents and tourists alike could experience the beauty of the area and spend some of their hard-earned dollars on rest and relaxation. The Exposition Company bought 175 acres of the McClure Farm for $8,500 and began developing the site. Unlike the modern conception of an amusement park, the company wished to create an exposition park, which would feature a summer-long county fair–type atmosphere enhanced by Chautauqua-esque lectures, education and political gatherings.

Cottages, hotels, broad avenues, shade trees, a 1,600-seat auditorium and exposition buildings were constructed to meet these lofty goals. Exceeding the luxury of most structures of that time, the park also featured running water, electric lights, its own post office, telegraph office, phone service and express service. Spending a summer at Conneaut Lake was akin to stepping to another world wholly dedicated to relaxation and fun. Exposition Park was dedicated on August 15, 1892, as one of the few of its kind to predate the World's Columbian Exposition in Chicago the next year. Conneaut Lake, Pennsylvania, was truly ahead of its time.

As the reputation of the park grew, so did investors' interest in the site. The railroad that would become the Bessemer and Lake Erie constructed a track that led directly into the park as its last stop. Eventually, the railroad became a shareholder, then lessee and later even operator of the park. Up to sixteen packed trains per day could be seen carting people in from all over Western Pennsylvania.

Guests would disembark and check in at one of the many glamorous hotels available to them, such as the Exposition Hotel, which opened in 1893. Although the park installed its first mechanical ride, the carousel, in 1899, owners were determined to keep the familial, community atmosphere rather than switch to the thrill-ride concept to which other

Postcard from Conneaut Lake Park looking north from the Hotel Conneaut. *Photo by Dave "Riptheskull," Flickr, used with CC BY-ND 2.0 Creative Commons License, no changes made, https:// creativecommons.org/licenses/by-nd/2.0.*

Inside Exposition Park, later Conneaut Lake Park, 1909. *Library of Congress.*

parks were converting. The park continued to grow through the turn of the century and attracted people to listen to popular bands and orchestras and participate in dancing, horseracing, boating, swimming, lectures, billiards, bowling, baseball, golf, tennis and more—at least until tragedy struck in 1908.

On December 2, 1908, fire gutted the midway, dance pavilion and the majority of buildings on the north side of Park Avenue between Center and Lake Streets. In addition, the bowling alley and four hotels (the Bismark, Puritan, Park and Colonial) were all destroyed. However, like the phoenix rising from the ashes, the fire brought new life to Exposition Park.

Owners invested in the creation of new buildings and attractions for vacationers and groups from across the region. The twenty-thousand-square-foot Dreamland Ballroom was constructed along with a brand-new bowling alley, the New Scenic railway coaster ride (which eventually became the iconic Blue Streak Rollercoaster), a new carousel (which still operates at the park to this day), Circle Swing ride, a Ferris wheel and a toboggan slide. Group outing reservations to the park soared and became an essential part of the business.

Groups of all kinds booked their outings to Exposition Park and took advantage of high-class dining, such as at the Hotel Virginia, which featured vermicelli soup, consommé clear, broiled blue pike and prime rib on its menu, as well as rustic tents and camp life all on the same grounds. Lodges, businesses, religious groups and political events were all held at the park, including a lively meeting of the Western Pennsylvania Undertakers Association that caught the attention of more than a few park attendees one evening. The staff at the hotel in which the association was residing

reported that the undertakers were seen "joy riding through the hotel in a casket propelled by fellow undertakers after sufficient imbibing." As unusual as this must have seemed, it was not the only attention-worthy event that occurred at the park.

In 1908, an annual Labor Day outing was held at Exposition Park by Republican, Democratic, Prohibitionist and Socialist groups from across Erie, Conneaut and Ashtabula. A debate was held between the men running for Pennsylvania state Senate from each party (with the exception of the Prohibitionist candidate, who did not show). The Erie Central Labor Union sponsored the debate, in which Republican Arthur L. Bates, Democrat John B. Brooks and Socialist Ralph Waldo Tillotson participated. Each man spoke for about thirty minutes to attendants regarding the "peculiar benefits held out by the platforms of the parties which they represented." The Socialist attendants must have enjoyed the setting of the debate, as their group returned in 1910 for another meeting.

On September 3, 1910, the Northwestern Pennsylvania Socialist group held a large meeting at Exposition Park and even boasted a famous speaker: Eugene V. Debs. Debs was a staunch Socialist who devoted the last twenty-five years of his life to "the development and dissemination of his ideas about Socialism and the labor movement." He did not advocate violence, held a committed antiwar stance and appealed to the virtues of organization and intelligence. Debs was about to run for president of the United States on the Socialist ticket in 1912 and likely used this meeting as not only an opportunity to speak on the importance of the workingman in America and the benefits of Socialism but also to make his case as to why he would be the best option for president. Although it is unknown exactly what Debs said at the meeting, it likely influenced the higher-than-average percentage of people who voted for him in 1912. In Crawford County, Debs achieved almost 9 percent of the vote and in Erie County almost 11 percent of the vote, while nationally

Lakefront view of Exposition Park, later Conneaut Lake Park, 1909. *Library of Congress.*

his average settled in around 6 percent. For a non–major party candidate, he performed quite well in Northwestern Pennsylvania. It would not be his last appearance at Exposition Park.

In June 1915, the Northwestern Pennsylvania Socialist Chautauqua chose to hold a large meeting of its membership at Exposition Park in Conneaut Lake. The meeting brought scores of people to the park from across Western Pennsylvania and beyond to take part in one of the largest encampments of Socialists ever held in this part of the state.

The event was advertised in newspapers all across Western Pennsylvania, encouraging people to reserve their tent and camping spot as soon as possible. The encampment was held from June 19 to June 28, 1915, and featured speakers of both state and national fame, including Reverend William Prosser, William F. Barnard, Gertrude Breslau Fuller, John W. Slayton, Mayor Walter Tyler, Edward Hayden, Lilith Martin and the vaunted Eugene Debs. The *Pittsburgh Press* advertised it to its readers by announcing, "Your attention is called to the big encampment at Conneaut Lake. Leagues from all over Western Pennsylvania will be present.…Eugene V. Debs, the foremost speaker of this country, will be the speaker."

Although the aforementioned speakers, likely with the exception of Debs, may not be familiar to the memories of readers today, they certainly were lauded and their speeches much anticipated in 1915. Edward Hayden was one of Pennsylvania's delegates to the Convention of the Socialist Party, and Walter Tyler was the first Socialist elected to town administration in Pennsylvania when he served from 1912 to 1915 as mayor of New Castle. Upon his election, the *New Castle News* noted that "the *News* opposed Mr. Tyler's election from the

outset, not because of any personal dislike for the candidate, but because the party whose candidate he was is a menace to the welfare of our entire country," but it would be fair to him in the future.

John W. Slayton was Tyler's campaign manager for the race and was active in the carpenter's trade union and even ran for governor in 1910. Slayton eventually served on city council and drew great acclaim for his debating and public speeches defending the tenets of Socialism.

Aside from Debs, the two most famous speakers at the Socialist encampment were the two women: Lilith Martin and Gertrude Breslau Fuller.

When Lilith Martin spoke at Exposition Park, she was a young twenty-eight-year-old lecturer and organizer for the Socialist Party, which she had joined only five years earlier. She spoke mostly about how Socialism would provide rights for women and children and was committed to their welfare. Martin eventually married L. Birch Wilson in 1921, and the next year she became the first woman to run for governor of Pennsylvania, just two years after women's right to vote was ratified. Although she lost the election, she won the votes of twenty thousand Pennsylvanians and made a strong statement for the rights of women in the commonwealth. Despite not attaining the office of governor, Martin did not give up on her goals of elected office. In 1930, she became the first Socialist woman to be elected to a legislative body in the United States by serving in the Pennsylvania state legislature. She was reelected in 1932 and again in 1934 before dying barely past the age of fifty in 1937. One of Martin's stops on her march to fame was at the 1915 encampment at Conneaut Lake.

Another famous Socialist woman who spoke to followers at Exposition Park that summer day in 1915 was Gertrude Breslau Fuller, a leading writer and speaker for the Socialist Party. Like Martin, Fuller was both a Socialist and a suffragist, strongly speaking out in favor of women's rights, particularly

Photo of the Bessemer and Lake Erie Railroad going through Greenville, Pennsylvania, sixteen miles south of Conneaut Lake. *Historic American Engineering Record, Jet Lowe, photographer, 1968.*

the right to vote. In 1907, she became a national organizer for the party and became famous for her highly intelligent political lectures. Having her at the Conneaut Lake encampment was nothing short of a major achievement for the Northwestern Pennsylvania Socialists.

Just before Fuller spoke in Crawford County, she gave a speech in Pittsburgh that likely would mirror her speech at Exposition Park. The *Pittsburgh Gazette Times* reported that at a public rally on May 2, 1915, Fuller pointed at the crowd and pronounced, "Why should the woman who earns a living for herself and her family be differentiated from the male wage earner? She pays the same rent, she pays the same price for food, for fuel, for clothing. Why should she not be allowed the privilege accorded men to have a voice in legislative affairs that she can better her condition? She is just as much qualified to vote as the men and the time has come when she will not be denied her rights." Fuller later joined the Democratic Party and served as the party's state vice-chairman before her death in Pittsburgh in 1952.

When Martin and Fuller spoke to the large Socialist encampment of men, women and children at Exposition Park on Conneaut Lake in 1915, women could not even legally cast their vote at the polls. Yet both were already famous political speakers and invigorated people across Pennsylvania regarding the future of the labor movement, Socialism and their rights in a rapidly changing nation.

As the nation was changing, so too was the setting of the 1915 encampment. Exposition Park was renamed Conneaut Lake Park in 1919 when the focus turned from the county fair aesthetic to a more amusement park orientation. Many mechanical rides were added, and the park experienced its own rollercoaster of ownership, financial difficulties and rebirth. Fortunately, it still operates today and has retained an aura of the communal exposition feeling on which it was founded more than 120 years ago. Exposition/Conneaut Lake Park was the gathering place for many people, groups and organizations throughout its history. It was a home away from home for everyone from unabashed undertakers to nationally recognized political figures in a picturesque place in rural Crawford County where the crystal blue water meets the land.

Worshipping бог: Carpatho-Rusyns in Northwestern Pennsylvania

Gud, Gott, Dia, Khristos or бог. All of these words mean the same thing, and it is a thread by which a great portion of residents in Northwestern Pennsylvania are tied: God. Given Pennsylvania's diversity of industry and proximity to the eastern seaboard, the commonwealth has been shaped immeasurably by immigrants from all over the world. No natural-born American, except those of Native American heritage, can trace his or her family lines back in time without crossing one of the oceans. We all come from somewhere else, and Northwestern Pennsylvania was a prime area for mixing the melting pot.

People of diverse nationalities and faiths made the pilgrimage to America and eventually called this corner of the state home. One needn't look far to see the embrace of heritage, such as through the ethnic festivals of food, culture and community held throughout the year across the region. German festivals, Greek gatherings, Irish pubs and Catholic churches dot the landscape and come easily to mind when considering culture and heritage in the area. Often forgotten are the families who can trace their lineage farther eastward, to a mountainous land where hardship and struggle lived simultaneously with love and devotion to family and faith.

In the late nineteenth and early twentieth centuries, a community of Carpatho-Rusyns from the Carpathian Mountains of Eastern Europe developed in Crawford and Erie Counties, and it still thrives there today. Countless communities fled to the United States to escape persecution in the hopes Lady Liberty would truly open her arms to the poor and huddled masses yearning to breathe free. Few were as homeless and tempest-tossed as the Carpatho-Rusyns, who were claimed by no country but persecuted by all.

The Carpatho-Rusyn people were and are a rural, village-bound people who subsisted on farming and were often chained to serfdom in the empires in which they were hemmed. Although they loved their land and had strong emotional ties to the soil, it was not prime farming property, and these mountain people performed backbreaking labor in order to survive. Due to constantly changing geopolitical boundaries, the Carpatho-Rusyn people were called by a variety of different names, including Rusyn, Rusnak, Uhro-Rusin, Ruthenian, Carpatho-Ukranian, Lemko, Slavish and Byzantine. Given its descriptive factor and encompassing of slight differences between groups of people, I will use the term Carpatho-Rusyn.

A great number of Carpatho-Rusyns were located in what was the kingdom of Hungary. Smaller numbers were in Poland and Ukraine, with others differentiating themselves as Subcarpathian Rus'. Hungary and Poland were both predominantly Roman Catholic. Since Carpatho-Rusyns followed the Eastern Orthodox religion, they were treated as second-class citizens economically, culturally and religiously, if given any status at all. Governments put immense pressure on the Carpatho-Rusyns to conform and convert or be destroyed through hunger and poverty.

This political pressure caused the creation of the Greek Catholic Church. In this version of the faith, Carpatho-Rusyns were allowed to keep practicing their Eastern rite liturgy (meaning the way they conducted services), Slavic language and cultural customs, but they had to recognize the pope in Rome as the head of the church instead of the Ecumenical Patriarch in Constantinople (now Istanbul). That system worked for a while, but resentment naturally festered and many Carpatho-Rusyn people desired to go back to their wholly Eastern faith.

Around the same time as political and religious turmoil was a drive to leave the land they loved. People were living hand-to-mouth, with only church and social life to sustain them. Young men, especially those who wished to avoid being forced to serve in the Austro-Hungarian army, began looking across the ocean for a new life. Poor land quality, poverty and military threats drove hundreds of thousands of Carpatho-Rusyn people to leave the land of their ancestors, often walking miles on craggy roads to the nearest train that would take them to an ocean liner that would hopefully deliver salvation.

More than 500,000 Carpatho-Rusyns endured the tumultuous and sickening four-week journey in steerage to arrive at the shores of the United States. Upon landing, these Eastern Europeans with complicated Slavic names were renamed by immigration officers, physically assessed and granted entry into a world of mixed fortune. They were former farmers, illiterate unskilled workers, unable to speak English and ripe for manipulation and abuse by unscrupulous businessmen.

Carpatho-Rusyns in the United States went from farmers to factory workers, usually performing the most dangerous and arduous labor in coal mines, salt mines and assembly lines. Because they could not speak English or read and write, these immigrants received a small portion of a normal wage and tended to live in communities surrounded by fellow immigrants. To add insult to injury, fellow workers and community members who did not like working or living with Eastern European Slavs would refer to them as "Hunkies," pejoratively referencing their Hungarian homeland. City life was vastly different than what they were used to, and most intended to return to their homeland with the fortunes they made in the United States. While this did happen, increasing numbers of people were stuck in a new vicious cycle of labor, poverty and drink. After World War I, it was even harder to return home and next to impossible to reunite with one's family given the quota system and the prejudicial undesirability of Eastern European immigrants.

In their desire to return to their roots and heed the heart's call to farming, Carpatho-Rusyn immigrants moved from cities in eastern Pennsylvania and eastern Ohio to the more rural, undeveloped land that was ripe for cultivation. Eastern European immigrants began a chain migration to an area steeped in Irish and German culture from a previous wave of immigrants. Rural Pennsylvania became dotted with "strange-looking gilded domes topped by equally unusual multi-barred crosses," signifying the arrival of the Eastern rite people. A little Ruthenia was developed in the largely uncharted territory of Erie and Crawford Counties; a quiet surge of Orthodox people was planting its roots in about 1,600 acres of Penn's Woods.

Creating a home away from home was not simple. This small community of people had divisions between them even in the homeland, disagreeing about the celibacy of the clergy, which languages to speak during the liturgy, which calendar to abide by, which countries to politically support and more. In America, leaders in the Catholic Church tried to forbid the

Eastern Orthodox Cross in the Saints Peter and Paul Garden, September 2018. *Courtesy of the author.*

Greek Catholics from practicing the Eastern rites and refused to allow them Eastern-born bishops, which created immense dissention. Churches were created along certain points of view, and competing churches sprang up from the dissenters. An example of this can be seen in Northwestern Pennsylvania through the Crossingville and Pageville Orthodox Churches.

The church in Pageville, just west of Edinboro and north of Crossingville, was founded in 1916 by Jacob Korchinsky, the famous priest who worked his mission in the United States before being one of the more than 1 million people tragically executed under the orders of Josef Stalin during the Soviet Terror. The St. Nicholas Church in Pageville operated, and operates, under the representation of the Moscow Patriarchate. It is a patriarchal parish and desired to stay under the administration of Moscow. The church is governed by the patriarch of Moscow in Russia through the administration of the vicar bishop. Not all immigrants and their American-born families wished to be under the tutelage of the Muscovites. Thus, the church in Crossingville, just a short five minutes south, was born.

Saints Peter and Paul Orthodox Church was founded under the archdiocese of Pittsburgh and the Orthodox Church of America in 1921. The story goes that in 1920, the last straw between competing factions was a dispute about the tone of the cantor during the liturgy and a segment that wished to form a new church broke away. The faithful were spread across the rural farmland of Erie and Crawford Counties and had little money with which to build a church from scratch. At first, they met and worshipped in people's homes, and then in a space above the Cussewago Inn/Kira's Store, before buying an old Lutheran Church in 1928 with a pooled $300.

For these newly minted Carpatho-Rusyn Americans, church was a "place of refuge in the midst of an alien environment, an undisturbed corner of the old country in the midst of the new." Although some still longed for the green fields of home, first-generation Americans became the bridge between cultures and helped create a fulfilling life in a new land.

In 1929, trustees Andrew Duke, Charles Kelyman and George Sheptak led a fledgling congregation in the purchase of land on which to assemble their new church. The Lutheran church they purchased was dismantled and the pieces labeled. They were then carted by horse and wagon to their new home miles away to be rebuilt as an Orthodox church. Members painstakingly rebuilt the structure, and the first Divine Liturgy was held on April 7, 1931, by Father Michael Zakan. Other parts of the church were built later by devout members, such as the iconostasis and parish home built by Carpatho-Rusyn immigrant Nicholas Olynik. Orthodox faith was

Left: St. Nicholas Orthodox Church in Pageville, Pennsylvania, just down the road from Saints Peter and Paul Orthodox Church, September 2018. *Courtesy of the author.*

Below: Nick Sekel's father's, John (Janos) Sekel, World War I draft registration card. The card shows that Sekel was a farmer and that he called Czechoslovakia home. *U.S. National Archives and Records Administration, 1917–18.*

Right: Saints Peter and Paul
Orthodox Church, Crossingville,
Pennsylvania, September 2018.
Courtesy of the author.

Below: Close-up view of Saints
Peter and Paul Orthodox Church
entryway, September 2018.
Courtesy of the author.

the anchor of their lives for these poor farming families. When times were tough, the community held strong.

One of these community members was born on the Sekel farm on Eureka Road in November 1927. Nicholas Sekel was one of five children born to Czechoslovakian immigrants Janos and Maria Pekuch Sekel. Janos was born in Vyslava, Sarissa Zupa, Slovakia, in July 1885. He first came to the United States in 1906, worked for a while and then returned home. In 1908, he was drafted and served in the Austro-Hungarian cavalry until 1912. Maria was born in the same area in 1895 and married Janos in an arranged marriage at the age of fifteen. The couple had a daughter, Anna, in Czechoslovakia in 1912. Janos retuned to the United States shortly after and was able to bring Maria and Anna to join him around 1920.

Janos first worked in the salt mines near Cleveland until he was able to join friend Michael Chaklos in rural Northwestern Pennsylvania, where a community of Carpatho-Rusyn farmers was forming. As difficult as farm labor was, it was much more desirable than the dangerous work in the mines. Janos, who went by John, and Maria, who went by Mary, moved with Anna to Eureka Road in Edinboro and set up a farmstead. The family had four more children: John Jr., Mary, Mike and Nick. The children were born at home with the help of a midwife named Lukashka, as were most babies were in rural areas. At home, the family spoke Slovak, or "our way" of speaking. Maria could speak very little English, and Janos learned through interactions with neighbors and merchants. Anna was taught English at school, and the children helped their mother with some English words.

During the Great Depression, the Sekel family fell on hard times. Bankruptcy rocked the household in 1937, and they were unable to hold on to their farm. After their situation improved, they moved in 1939 to a new farm of 110 acres on Fry Road, where Nick and his wife, Theona, lived until her recent passing.

Nick grew up during the heyday of Carpatho-Rusyn culture in Northwestern Pennsylvania. As a small child, he was surrounded by family, friends and neighbors who shared in his culture and faith. He estimates

Sekel family census record, 1930. Nick Sekel is listed on the bottom line. *U.S. Census Bureau.*

that there were about fifty Orthodox families in the Crossingville area and fourteen in Cambridge Springs, each with a large pack of children. Traveling on dirt paths with no cars and in the challenging Northwestern Pennsylvania weather was not easy, especially with a coterie of children in tow. Thus, families did not often travel, and neighbors got to know one another well and came to depend on one another for support and camaraderie.

Fortunately for Nick, within a three-mile radius of their home lived about fifteen Orthodox families with four or five boys per family, creating an easy atmosphere for friends. The Sekel family, like most, were poor and lived on subsistence farming. They were fed but had little spending money. At one time, their farm was home to eight cows, two hundred chickens, ducks, geese, pigs and rabbits, as well as fields full of cabbage and potatoes. After church on Sundays, the family would always cook a large chicken or beef dinner. Meals usually featured noodles, cabbage, potatoes, latkes, rice, goulash, sauerkraut and gallons upon gallons of different kinds of soup.

Food is a staple of Carpatho-Rusyn culture. Holidays are hallmarked by worship followed by luscious meals in celebration. At Easter, or Pascha, a midnight service is held on Good Friday that usually lasts over three hours. It is capped by a symbolic walk around the church. On Easter Sunday, the resurrection celebration begins in full. The end of Lent and the resurrection of Иисус Христос (pronounced "ee-soos krees-tos"), or Jesus Christ, is celebrated in church and at home with friends and family. In Centerville, Pennsylvania, a Russian Orthodox family originally from Philipsburg, Pennsylvania, carried on these traditions and passed them down to their children and grandchildren.

In contrast to the families of the Saints Peter and Paul Orthodox Church in Crossingville who were able to create an entire community, in more far-flung areas where fewer people shared their culture and faith, Carpatho-Rusyns celebrated their traditions alone. Faith Fetcenko was born to Carpatho-Rusyn parents George and Anna Bodenshok Fetcenko in Hawk Run, Pennsylvania, in 1936. The Fetcenko and Bodenshok families were devout members of the St. John the Baptist Russian Orthodox Church in Chester Hill, whose lineage is traced to the Prešov region of modern-day Slovakia. Eventually, Fetcenko married Michael Hilburn, a convert from Denham Springs, Louisiana, had a son and moved to Northwestern Pennsylvania. After generations of deep roots, Carpatho-Rusyn traditions now had to be maintained without the support of a church family.

One of the major ways these traditions were kept alive was through food. Paska, the Easter "bread of life"; Hren, a spicy concoction of beets and horseradish; Hrutka, an Easter cheese that contains no actual cheese; and Zaprhashka, the Eastern European take on a roux mixed with beans, were laboriously made every year, tying the family to their ethnic and religious roots. When their son, John, married Heather Sterling, a Catholic woman of Irish and German heritage from ten miles down the road, no Fetcenko ancestors could have prophesied that she would create arguably the best Russian Orthodox food in Northwestern Pennsylvania (and in the world, in the opinion of this author).

Foodways traditions have been passed down in Carpatho-Rusyn families for generations through handwritten cookbooks, time-honored recipes and small tidbits of advice tweaked over years of experimentation and feasting. Stained, well-loved family cookbooks are sprinkled with notes in the margins about which ingredients are essential, which can be substituted, how to extract maximum flavor and even which stores carried hard-to-find ingredients. Carptho-Rusyn culture and Orthodox faith have been kept alive in Rusyn kitchens across the commonwealth and especially in Northwestern Pennsylvania.

Rusyns were wont to eat their fill of traditional foods due to their lifetimes of hard blue-collar work. Whether they were farming, taking care of animals, cleaning, cooking or going to school, each member of the family earned his or her keep and worked for everything they had. In 1937, something finally arrived in this rural area that Nick Sekel described as the best thing that ever happened to his family: electricity.

When electricity finally appeared in rural Erie and Crawford Counties, it was a game-changer for rural families. Indoor plumbing, lighting and power were suddenly possible, easing the burden enormously. Electricity also created new opportunities. Nick decided to assist the one man sent by the electric company to run wire. He learned the trade, and when he went into the navy, he worked as an electrician. Later in his career, he picked up the skill again and retired from Meadville Medical Center as an electrician in 1992.

Throughout his life, Nick and the Sekel family have been instrumental in the development of the Saints Peter and Paul Orthodox Church. As one of the oldest members of the congregation, Nick can remember the early history and compare it to the evolution of the faith and where the church stands today. He has noticed that churchgoing families have experienced attrition, going from about 150 parishioners in 1980s to between 40 and 50 adults on a good Sunday. He attributes this to more interfaith marriages and a general societal move away from organized religion.

The Orthodox Church, like many churches in the twenty-first century, is going through tough times. However, for this more than one-thousand-year-old religion, it is not the first period of strife. Although the church struggles, the faith remains strong. Eastern Orthodox people have endured persecution, execution and poverty and emerged reborn and stronger than ever. They know in their souls how to survive the tests of struggle. In the opinions of some followers, decreasing factionalism and fundamentalism could help to reunite and grow the religion. Regardless of the future of organized Eastern Orthodoxy in Northwestern Pennsylvania, Carpatho-Rusyn culture remains alive in the hearts and homes of second-, third-, fourth- and even fifth-generation immigrants whose ancestors were welcomed by the lifted lamp beside the golden door.

CHAPTER 5

STRIKING CLEAR GOLD

The Northwestern Pennsylvania Mineral Water Bonanza

VITAMINS ON THE VERANDA: THE RIVERSIDE INN

Rural Northwestern Pennsylvania is mainly famous for one very important 1859 discovery: oil, just outside Titusville. However, oil is not the only substance for which the region drew acclaim in the nineteenth and early twentieth centuries. Water, the region's clear gold as opposed to the black gold of oil, was found to be full of vitamins and minerals that purportedly created positive health benefits for those that drank it or bathed in it. Multiple towns took advantage when a lucky person stumbled across one of these lucrative springs and created businesses and sometimes even entire town reputations based on the pleasing water. The first of these exciting finds happened in Crawford County, slightly south of the Erie County line.

While Edwin Drake was in the midst of drilling the first commercial oil well twenty-seven miles away, another Crawford County pioneer was discovering his own life-changing substance. Dr. Joseph Gray discovered a spring of clear, cool water on his property that year and found the taste to be magnificent. Although the spring was wonderful, Dr. Gray did not give much more thought to it until more than twenty years later in 1884.

Before Gray stumbled across his intriguing spring in the northwestern corner of Crawford County, Cummingstown had been inhabited since 1822. It was incorporated as the borough of Cambridge in 1866 and, due to the fame of Gray's water, was renamed in 1897 and has been known as Cambridge Springs ever since.

The Riverside Hotel near the original springs in Cambridge Springs, Pennsylvania. *Map by T.M. Fowler and James B. Moyer, 1895.*

Gray traveled to Hot Springs, Arkansas, and while there, observed other waters and concluded that mineral water must contain medicinal properties given its seeming ability to heal those who consumed it. In 1877, Gray opened a sanitarium to offer his mineral water to wealthy vacationers and modeled his business on the southern mineral water companies he experienced. Although he knew the potential of mineral water, he probably did not know the heights his success would reach, as mineral water was quickly becoming a hot commodity in Northwestern Pennsylvania.

The 1902 edition of *Cutter's Guide* described how "[p]eople came in small numbers at first, but after a few years the numbers of invalid visitors seeking relief by drinking these waters became so great that large hotels were demanded for their accommodation and this demand is yet on the increase."

Cambridge gained popularity through "the many cures made by drinking the mineral waters from these springs," which caused hotels and boardinghouses to be built and the population to increase. Many hotels sprang up as a result of the mineral water industry, creating a name for the borough of Cambridge in many wealthy circles. Mineral waters were in high demand by wealthy travelers, and men and women indulged themselves by retreating from cities across the nation to sanitariums and mineral springs.

While there, respite and relaxation in the form of delicious meals, lounging on porches and drinking gallons of spring water were achieved by visitors causing local businesses to flourish.

One of the most famous hotels to capitalize on the mineral water industry opened in 1877, the Hotel Riverside. This hotel was first a sanitarium, but vacationers were more open to the draw of a luxurious hotel. A three-story building that featured wide hallways and expansive rooms, the Hotel Riverside boasted a beautiful view regardless of the season. *Cutter's Guide* explained that the hotel was built like a sanitarium but without the "unpleasant features." Instead, the hotel had a meeting room, easy chairs and rocking chairs, writing tables, a parlor, a music room and even a "great old-fashioned fireplace that bid defiance to cold." Bedrooms were located on the first, second and third floors and were eventually lit with electricity and heated with steam.

Until William D. Rider of Franklin purchased the hotel and secured the spring and farm lease from Dr. Gray in 1890, the Hotel Riverside had only modest success. After the ownership change, the hotel found new life. Rider enlarged the structure and built a casino, bottling works, barn and boardwalk to the spring, about a quarter mile away. He also rebuilt the springhouse, added a produce garden and acquired horses. The Gray family offered to sell the spring to Rider for $60,000 after Gray's death in 1891, but he declined. Despite enlarging the holdings and increasing the popularity of the business, Rider was not the best steward. After many nasty fights with stockholders and partners, Rider was forced to sell the property by court-ordered arbitration in 1894.

Soon after, the Hotel Riverside and all its additions were purchased by William Baird Sr. and his wife, Elizabeth Baird, of Pittsburgh for $75,000. Elizabeth had previously stayed at the hotel and consumed its health-giving waters. She greatly enjoyed her time there, to the point that when it came up for sale, she and her husband decided to be the new owners. Unlike Rider, the Bairds took the Grays up on their offer and purchased the spring and farm for $60,000. In 1897, Rider would go on to open a competing hotel, the Hotel Rider, which also featured mineral spring water as its major draw.

The Hotel Riverside could hold up to three hundred guests who were attracted by the water and stayed for the entertainment. The casino in the hotel featured billiards and bowling, as well as dancing and an amusement hall. Vacationers would spend their days drinking between nine and fifty-four glasses of the special mineral water while playing games, dancing or just

The Gray Springs Boardwalk in Cambridge Springs, Pennsylvania. *Map by T.M. Fowler and James B. Moyer, 1895.*

The Hotel Rider overlooking all of Cambridge Springs. *Map by T.M. Fowler and James B. Moyer, 1895.*

enjoying the scenery. For those who were feeling more adventurous, the hotel also offered aquatic sports such as canoeing, boating, skiffs and swimming.

The Bairds took full advantage of everything Rider had acquired plus the new addition of the Gray Farm. They created a gardens, greenhouses and hotbeds that grew seasonal foods to be harvested and served at the hotel. The Bairds also cultivated seasonal game, fruit and even a herd of cattle, which produced milk and cream for guests.

For two to three dollars per day for transient guests or ten to seventeen dollars per week for permanent guests, the Hotel Riverside could provide a relaxing atmosphere, great food, excursions and mineral water baths. The hotel featured a variety of baths, including Turkish, Russian, cabinet, electric, sea-salt, mineral, plunge, shower and needle baths. Despite all these attractions, the main pull to the area remained the curative properties of the potable mineral water. *Cutter's Guide* described the waters from firsthand experience:

> [The springs were] *clear and sparkling as champagne* [and were made up of a] *compound of minerals…particularly valuable in the cure of rheumatism, gout, constipation, indigestion, malaria, nervous prostration, bilious derangement, catarrhal conditions of the bladder and kidneys, diabetes and Bright's disease.*
>
> *Unlike most medicinal waters, you do not have to learn to like it. The first draught is refreshing and palatable. It is a tonic without reaction. It is quickly assimilated and may be taken in quantities sufficiently large to flush and cleanse the system without any inconvenience.*
>
> *The spring is but a short distance from the Riverside Hotel, and is connective with it by an elevated boardwalk, lighted by electricity. It is the water from this spring, "the old, original," it is called, that has proved of the greatest benefit to those seeking health.*
>
> *The spring is covered by a very comfortable pavilion, furnished with plenty of lounging seats. The attendants at the spring pass the clear, sparkling water up to visitors, among whom there is plenty of fun and rivalry over the amount of water that can be taken. Those who are under regular treatment, however, have their drinking schedule made out by the house physician, to which they adhere strictly.*

Though arguably the most famous, the Riverside Hotel was not the only institution to capitalize on the popularity of spring water in the late nineteenth century. Other Cambridge Springs hotels also included the

Detailed map of Cambridgeboro, Pennsylvania, which would later be renamed Cambridge Springs. *Map by T.M. Fowler and James B. Moyer, 1895.*

previously mentioned Hotel Rider, the Petticord Mineral Springs, Magnesia Spring, the New Cambridge Hotel, the Hotel Kelly, Shady Lawn, the National Hotel and the Todd Sanitarium and Bath House. As time soldiered on, it became more and more difficult for Cambridge Springs getaways to survive when their existence was predicated on mineral water in a rural setting off the beaten path.

A new mass-produced invention began to spell doom for rural health resorts at the turn of the century. While in the nineteenth century, foot (whether human or horse) and train were the only ways to travel in Crawford County, ownership of automobiles was growing. In order to combat the newfound transience allowed by automobiles, the Bairds built a golf course to entice vacationers to plan longer stays. Unfortunately, their efforts were stalled by a lawsuit by the United States government in 1916 that exposed the artificial side of the mineral water business.

The U.S. Department of Agriculture sued the Bairds under the auspices of the Pure Food and Drug Act of 1906 for misbranding their mineral water as "bottled at the source" when it was bottled a quarter mile from the source and for advertising it as "pure spring water" when it was artificially carbonated. In addition, the mineral water was advertised with claims to cure a litany of ailments that the government said were not supported with medical evidence. The Bairds complied, changed their branding and paid a twenty-dollar fine.

Just five years after this episode, William Baird died, leaving a great legacy at the Riverside Hotel. Under his ownership, Baird had turned their small 7-acre purchase into a sprawling 435-acre estate. The property stayed in the hands of the family and Baird's son, William, and two daughters, Nettie and Lillian. The Baird family was very politically and socially active in the community. The Pittsburgh transplants donated to the local school, which eventually named the athletic field Baird Field, and bequeathed $100,000 to build a library.

In 1946, the Baird children sold the estate to the Incas Company of Pittsburgh. Colonel Francis W. Parke, veteran of World Wars I and II, was named operator and William Baird Jr. as advisor. Parke reshaped the marketing so that the Riverside could be open year-round. He created winter vacation packages, including ice skating on the new ice rink, skijoring (skiing while pulled by a horse, dog or car), tobogganing, trap shooting and sleigh rides. The mineral water days had come to an end, and the hotel struggled to find its footing in the post-water world.

After Parke's leadership, the property changed hands numerous times, but it remained open as the Riverside Inn. In 1979, Gray Mineral Water made

Photograph of the Riverside Inn, taken on July 31, 2011. It would burn only six years later, losing a century of rich architectural history. *From Niagara, Wikimedia Commons, July 31, 2011, Creative Commons License CC by 3.0, https://creativecommons.org/licenses/by/3.0.*

a comeback when it was bottled and sold commercially with government approval by Saegertown Ginger Ale Company.

After more than 130 years of perseverance, the Riverside Inn was unable to survive one last challenge in May 2017. In the early morning hours of May 2, 2017, a fire broke out in the kitchen of the hotel and quickly spread. Everyone escaped without harm, but the stately building was not so lucky. Within hours, the old building was consumed by flame. Firefighters worked tirelessly to quell the flames licking the wood without success. News crews poured in, and heartbroken spectators filled the street and parking lot, watching helplessly as a beloved landmark disappeared. Although the Riverside Inn no longer stands as a testament to the importance of the mineral water industry in Cambridge Springs, its legacy lives on in the name that says it all.

Fieldmore Springs and the Pleasantville Gusher

The mineral water spectacle in Cambridge Springs was a draw for almost fifty years, while residents of southeastern Crawford County were clamoring for a different kind of lucrative substance. Instead of clear gold, they hungered for black gold: oil. Dr. Joseph Gray and Colonel Edwin Laurentine Drake discovered their respective wells in the same year, but Titusville did not climb aboard the mineral water train for decades. Finally, just after the turn of the century, a different doctor came upon a delicious spring just southeast of the city and created a competitor for the springs of Cambridge.

While most people still flocked to Titusville for oil, a little-known gusher up the hill just east of Titusville was also attracting quite a bit of attention. In 1906, Dr. S.N. Burchfield built a business on the back of the clear, cool streams running on his new property slightly over the border into Venango County, Pennsylvania.

The year before, Dr. Burchfield came to the Titusville area to pioneer a kind of hotel very popular at the time called a sanitarium. Today, we would classify most of these dwellings as health resorts or health spas, although they also attracted many who were suffering physical ills in need of treatment more than just relaxation. Burchfield paid an enormous undisclosed sum to build the great estate he would name Fieldmore Springs. Supposedly using all native stone and brick, the massive building was constructed in 1906

Postcard of the Fieldmore Springs Hotel, located between Titusville and Pleasantville. *Weiler Publishing Company.*

beside man-made ponds and lakes to beautify the grounds. The business—called a hotel, sanitarium and health resort throughout its history—was easily accessible for patrons, as it was located conveniently on the trolley car line to Titusville.

In June 1907, the *Titusville Herald* explained the genesis of the resort, writing, "The erection of the hotel was made possible by the discovery of a vein of perfect drinking water. About five years ago [1902] oil well drillers tapped a subterranean river which flowed through the casing from a depth of about a hundred feet. The water has been submitted to several analyses. It is pronounced perfect in every respect. It is believed and in fact known to contain curative agents for many diseases, especially those of the stomach and kidneys." The hotel was designed to appeal to "overworked men and women of Pittsburgh, Buffalo, Cleveland, and elsewhere who wish a quiet, wholesome place to spend a few weeks."

Fieldmore Springs opened on Saturday, June 15, 1907, to great acclaim. Between eight hundred and one thousand people toured the hotel and experienced the ornate decoration and furnishings at the opening event. Visitors could see that the front hall was connected to a parlor and led up to a dining room on the second floor. Each room was adorned with hardwood floors, modern ventilation and open balconies with beautiful views. The building even had an elevator that reached every floor and a telephone in each room.

The hotel stood five stories tall and boasted seventy-five suites that could house between 100 and 150 guests. The first managers were Mr. and Mrs. W. Crosby, who helped excitedly greet guests on opening day. The *Titusville Herald* described how "[t]he hotel is approached from the street railway line by a wide cement walk, boarded by potted plants and flowers and dividing at the near approach of the structure to accommodate a fine fountain twenty feet in diameter." The fountain was stocked with twenty large trout, and a stream was used to create several miniature lakes and waterfalls for patrons to relax near and enjoy.

In addition to its green spaces, the health resort also featured a bowling alley, billiards, a grill and bar, a farm and a greenhouse, similar to that of the Hotel Riverside in Cambridge Springs. Surrounding the resort were one hundred acres of pine and hemlock forest, allowing the sick to be enveloped by fresh air and healing waters. The *Titusville Herald* proclaimed, "There is no more beautiful spot in the foothills of the Alleghenies than Fieldmore."

Immediately after opening, Fieldmore Springs began catering to patients as well as hosting parties and club meetings. The Titusville Woman's Club

This distance view of the Fieldmore Springs Hotel was featured on a postcard for guests to send home to their loved ones, circa 1908. *Postcard by Cohn & Oakleaf, Titusville, Pennsylvania.*

held its meeting at the hotel that very week. In 1908, a huge gala was hosted at the site in honor of famous local oilman Joseph Seep's seventieth birthday, garnering attention from all over the region.

Fieldmore Springs continued operating successfully for many years until Venango County's Judge Criswell declared the county dry in April 1914, six years before national Prohibition. Because a good portion of Fieldmore Springs's business was dependent on liquor sales, this proclamation, followed by more than a decade of Prohibition, negatively affected the hotel moreso than other hotels with more established mineral water reputations.

Eventually, the building and land were sold to another doctor and established as the Bashline-Shrum Osteopathic Clinic in 1941. Dr. M.F. Bashline and his wife, nurse Alberta Shrum Bashline, lived at the clinic and offered "minor surgery, plasmatic therapy, octozone therapy, needle surgery, care for hemorrhoids, hernias, and colonic irrigations," continuing the health ethos of the property.

Unfortunately, on January 22, 1947, the coldest morning of the winter, Fieldmore Springs was doomed to the same fate that would befall the Riverside seventy years in the future. As the temperature dropped, the building caught fire and burned to the ground. All six patients were evacuated safely, but the main building was badly damaged. The ponds that normally would have quelled the fire had run dry, and it was learned that instead of being built from stone as originally purported, the building was built entirely from wood, the brick only being a veneer.

Over the next half century, the land was used a variety of ways. In 1951, Titusville residents purchased the one-hundred-plus acres in the hopes of using the land for public recreation such as camping, horseback riding and a game preserve. From the 1950s through the 1960s, the remaining buildings became the Bashline Rest Home and, in 1972, the Paradise Valley Home. The property changed hands in 1974, becoming Titusville Dry Goods. In March 1994, Connie Phillips purchased what was left of the buildings and created the Fieldmore Springs Antique Emporium. Antiques were showcased in former patient rooms and operating areas. This business was active until September 2005, when it closed.

Staying at the Fieldmore Springs in its early years was a working person's respite from the hardships of the world. For two dollars a day (fifty-three dollars today), a person could rent a room and relax with the cooling mineral water of the springs and lazily gaze out onto the impeccably landscaped grounds. As one drives by, it is easy to imagine what it used to be—a rest stop for the weary in the heart of Northwestern Pennsylvania.

Corry Artesian Mineral Water Company: Erie County's Bid for Bottled Bubbly

Sumptuous mineral water was not exclusive to the southern region of Northwestern Pennsylvania. Clear waters could also be found flowing through the creeks, streams and wells of Erie County. In Corry, Pennsylvania, this clear tonic was taken advantage of by local Thomas Pine.

After Dr. Gray in Cambridge Springs but before Dr. Burchfield in Titusville came Thomas Pine in Corry. In 1886, Thomas Pine was digging a well for the "ordinary purposes" of simply finding drinking water when he stumbled on a reserve of water with striking properties. After drilling down 214 feet through solid rock, "a flowing well of water pleasing to the taste and clear as crystal was obtained. Its analysis proved it to be free from organic matter, pure and wholesome and rich in mineral properties. It retains all its constituents and does not deteriorate by standing."

By the 1890s, the well that produced the crystal-clear water had been built into a business called the Corry Artesian Mineral Water Company. Much of the business was managed by proprietor J. Hanford Duke, originally of Olean, New York. Duke was himself a patron of the company and found so much relief in his treatment and excitement about the product that he purchased the property and began developing it.

A springhouse was built over the well, and people could come and purchase water there. The facility was expanded into a three-story building with a great deal of furnishings for visitors to enjoy. The *Pharmaceutical Era* periodical visited the business in 1892, reporting how the business was laid out and the quality visitors could expect to enjoy.

The periodical stated that the basement contained the bottling and shipping works for outgoing cases of water. It went on to describe how "[t]he reception, smoke and well rooms are all on the first floor and are comfortably heated by steam. The well room is furnished with seats and around the curb are shelves filled with glasses from which to drink this delicious water as it gurgles up and flows forth freely for all who wish to avail themselves of its beneficial and curative properties." Above that floor, the second and third floors featured parlors and bedrooms that were made available to traveling guests who wished to indulge in the supposedly health-giving waters.

The reporter also tasted some of the water, including a sample that had been standing for more than six months to test the claim that even standing water at the well was delicious. He verified the claim, writing that "it was as fresh and sweet as when it came from the ground." Beyond drinking to

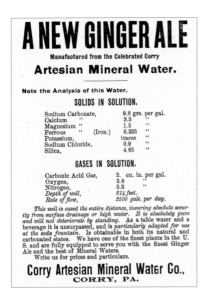

A NEW GINGER ALE

Manufactured from the Celebrated Corry

Artesian Mineral Water.

Note the Analysis of this Water.

SOLIDS IN SOLUTION.

Sodium Carbonate,	9.8 grs. per gal.	
Calcium "	3.5	"
Magnesium "	1.5	"
Ferrous " (Iron.)	0.235	"
Potassium,	traces	"
Sodium Chloride,	0.9	"
Silica,	4.65	"

GASES IN SOLUTION.

Carbonic Acid Gas,	2. cu. in. per gal.	
Oxygen,	2.8	"
Nitrogen,	5.2	"
Depth of well,	214 feet.	
Rate of flow,	2500 gals. per day.	

This well is cased the entire distance, insuring absolute security from surface drainage or high water. It is absolutely pure and will not deteriorate by standing. As a table water and a beverage it is unsurpassed, and is *particularly adapted for use at the soda fountain.* Is obtainable in both its natural and carbonated states. We have one of the finest plants in the U. S. and are fully equipped to serve you with the finest Ginger Ale and the best of Mineral Waters.

Write us for prices and particulars.

Corry Artesian Mineral Water Co.,
CORRY, PA.

Left: Corry Artesian Mineral Water Company Advertisement. *From the* Pharmaceutical Era, *May 15, 1892.*

Below: Bird's-eye view map of Corry, Pennsylvania, by T.M. Fowler and James Moyer from 1895. The Corry Artesian Mineral Water Company was featured as an important business by the mapmakers. *Library of Congress.*

cure internal ailments, the Corry Artesian Water was said to also be most desirable for bathing. The magazine reported that when bathing in Corry's water, "The flesh remains soft and moist for hours after bathing in it. Its curative properties in cases of stomach and kidney troubles have become widely known."

After capitalizing on the drinking and bathing aspects of the water, Duke focused on marketing the water to soda fountains and local businesses. He also expanded the bottling and shipping capabilities of the business, creating more plant space for the manufacture of ginger ale, for which "this water is particularly adapted," according to taste testers.

The Corry Artesian Mineral Water Company grew quickly at its location at the corner of West Smith and East Wayne Streets in the city of Corry. People came from far and wide to try out the bathhouses and mineral water as its popularity increased. Northwestern Pennsylvania was experiencing a water boom, like the oil boom that previously shook the region. Corry was very proud of its famous well and celebrated the company for marketing the purity and health-giving properties of the waters contained within. Modern conveniences were added to the large bathhouse and sleeping rooms that allowed visitors to extend their stays and enjoy the surrounding entertainments of the city and countryside in addition to the liquid relaxation.

Both visitors and locals alike could purchase this locally sourced water and its derivatives straight from the well or prebottled for $3.50 per case or utilize the bathhouse for $0.35.

Although the company seemed to be going strong, it, as with other sanitarium-like business models in the area, fell on hard times as the calendar flipped to the twentieth century. It persisted for fourteen years until 1914, when the buildings that had been so meticulously constructed to make the most out of the water business fatefully burned.

From Cambridge Springs to Titusville to Corry, Northwestern Pennsylvanians saw that clear gold was a strong, lucrative business for many pioneers who wished to strike out outside the realm of oil or heavy industry. The model of rest and relaxation through consuming and covering oneself in clear, cool, rurally sourced water appealed to vacationers, transient visitors and locals alike who patronized the various businesses that prided themselves on self-sustainment and cutting-edge accoutrements.

While Cambridge Springs was by far the most successful experiment in this vein, even leaving its mark on the name of the town, many train stops across the area saw the potential in marketing their getaways as curative for the ills of the modern world. Although not all, or even arguably most, of the various proprietors' claims were objectively true, they still remained successful for decades. The medicinal waters ruled Northwestern Pennsylvania for decades, claiming to cure everything from the common cold to deadly consumption, until they all fatefully met their ultimate match at the hand of the flame.

CHAPTER 6

OPIUM, OIL AND OREGON

Rural Medicine in NWPA

PISO'S CURE FOR CONSUMPTION

There were many things that could kill you in the Northwestern Pennsylvania wilderness in the nineteenth century. Fires, floods, snow, venomous bites, horses, trains, murder and more. But one of the most ravaging of all was contagious disease. When land tracts were being bought, trees timbered, oil wells sunk and businesses booming, people flooded into areas that were previously sparsely populated and did not have the infrastructure to support such a population increase. As a result, disease spread like wildfire. Victorians had no concept of germs, as Louis Pasteur's germ theory was still but a dream in his young French mind. People did not wash their hands, cover their coughs or sanitize instruments as we diligently do today. Disease was terrifying, and one of the most terrifying attacked the lungs, causing everyone from infants to the elderly to cough droplets of blood as they faded from this world.

Consumption is the Victorian-era term for a disease with many names: phthisis, "White Plague" or, most commonly today, tuberculosis. It was called consumption because of the all-consuming way the disease took over one's body and caused great weight loss and deterioration. In the nineteenth century, consumption forged an unfortunate reputation as a romantic disease, one that brought a person a "good death" as it was slow progressing and caused what was seen as pale-skinned beauty. Consumption represented purity, especially for the upper classes. Despite this social romanticism of the disease, dying from consumption was not a fate many would request.

Thousands of people across the United States were dying from consumption, whether they lived in tight, urban areas or in the outposts. Companies promoting "cures" for the disease popped up as an answer to people's desperation. Piso's Cure for Consumption filled this void in 1864 when it was sold by Ezra T. Hazeltine in Warren.

E.T. Hazeltine was born in 1836 just across the New York/Pennsylvania border in Busti, New York. He migrated to Warren in 1860 with his wife, Rachel, and met the man who changed his life forever: Micajah C. Talbott. Talbott was a doctor in Warren and had been experimenting with concoctions to treat the consumption he witnessed daily. The two teamed up with Myron Waters—a lumberman, oilman, refiner, railroad baron and president of Citizens National Bank—who bankrolled the operation and began selling their tonic, Piso's Cure for Consumption, in Hazeltine's new drugstore.

Piso's (pronounced "pie-soz") started as a small operation that grew its name through intense advertising. Hazeltine and Talbott placed advertisements in newspapers across Pennsylvania, including Warren, Bradford, Oil City, Titusville and even broader in Altoona, New Castle and Kittanning. They placed their images and branding on everything from

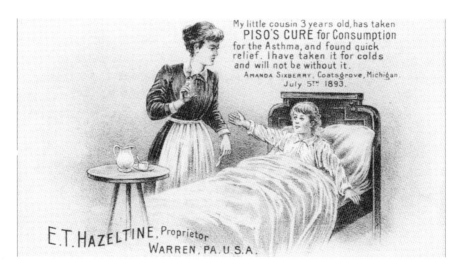

Piso's Cure for Consumption advertisement featuring a "testimonial" from a consumer. *Miami University Libraries Digital Collections, circa 1893.*

books to bicycle stands, tiny almanacs, puzzles, games and short stories. Their reputation ballooned. Piso's was flying off the shelves at twenty-five cents per bottle, even despite the odd name that the inventors never did seem to have a reason for choosing.

Hazeltine hired traveling salesmen to spread their formula across state lines. In need of greater production capabilities, in 1870 they moved the operation from the Johnson Block in Warren to "the Island," a literal island in the middle of the Allegheny River in Warren that was connected to land via bridge. The new factory made it so that the company could produce about twenty thousand bottles every day. In the post–Civil War era, most medicines had a very addictive ingredient, one that would come to dominate our cultural landscape now more than ever: opium.

The original formula for Piso's Cure for Consumption, and other tonics they made such as Piso's Catarrh Cure and Piso's Throat and Chest Salve, contained a large percentage of opium and morphine derivatives. Extremely addictive, though marketed as safe, opium was the major ingredient in a number of rural cures in the mid-nineteenth century. After legislation precluded the use of opium in tonics after 1872, Piso's substituted with cannabis, chloroform and alcohol instead. One addiction was simply replaced with another.

By 1894, the Piso Company was the largest employer in Warren. It marketed many of its products, such as Piso's Tablets, to women whom they proclaimed were overcome with "female diseases" and would rather "die by inches than consult anyone, even by letter, about their private troubles." Despite their sexism-riddled language, the company provided employment for scores of women in Warren, especially single women and those attempting to escape abusive relationships. In one case, a nineteen-year-old woman named Eva Stines fled to Warren from Dunkirk, New York, to escape the wrath of her husband and protect their two-year-old son. She said that she had been forced to marry him when she was only sixteen and that he threatened to kill her if she left. The Piso Company hired her, and she started immediately. The next day, forty-year-old John Stines arrived at the Piso plant, sought out his wife and shot her four times while her fifteen-year-old coworker fought him off. Amazingly, Eva fought through her injuries as John took his own life at the factory.

The Piso Company incorporated in 1894 under the auspices of original founders Ezra T. Hazeltine, William Talbott and Myron Waters, as well as new additions Henry M. Fisher and Henry Gerould. Their great success drove copycats, and they were even forced to sue a company in Cincinnati that used the very same bottle and wrapper as theirs, simply changing the name to "Pizo's" instead of "Piso's."

The company was one of Warren's signature industries, changing the landscape and the people in it. In October 1895, the *Warren Mail* described the rise of the tonic business, writing that "since its inauguration [Piso's] has experienced a wonderful growth in the volume of its trade. [Its] specific remedies have gained a high reputation and a large and steadily increasing demand all over the country….This medicine is pleasant to use and is highly recommended by some of the best physicians and most reliable business men and citizens. Testimonials of the highest character have been received from all over the world testifying to the wonderful cures affected by this cure." But the success could not last for much longer, for the government was sniffing out Hazeltine's cannabis-laden trail.

Starting in 1899, U.S. Congress, spurred by the Woman's Christian Temperance Union (WCTU), began investigating the ethics and veracity of mail-order cures. At the turn of the century, the company was forced to rename the product Piso's Cough Syrup, as it could no longer claim to "cure" consumption under the law. The company was struck another blow when in 1906 Congress passed the Pure Food and Drug Act, requiring a list of ingredients on the label. To battle the rising tide of bad publicity over its recipe, Piso's gave away patriotic items with its tonics to engender positive feelings. In 1907, the word *Cure* was replaced with *Remedy* before finally, in 1910, the Piso Company was formally sued by the federal government. The government stated that Piso's was "making false and misleading statements as to the contents of a medicine manufactured by it." Fines were levied, and the business paid, persevering as best it could.

In 1911, the company was under new management with Mary T. Fisher, sister of Dr. William Talbott, as president, Anna Frey as chief chemist, Etta Bridenbaker as assistant secretary and Mrs. Pixley as superintendent of advertising. Women were now running the show, and they went on an advertising blitz to reinvigorate the company. Cutting-edge assembly line technology was instituted by President Fisher, and she ramped up production in the pre-winter months in anticipation of cold weather demand. The company continued its bold advances in the newspapers, claiming the fact that the "medicine is safe to take and does not contain any habit-forming drugs has been established in the courts, and all who insist on Pure Foods and Drugs may find in Piso an efficacious remedy and a medicine without harmful ingredients." The main products then were Piso's Remedy, Piso's Catarrh Balm and Piso's Tooth Powder.

In March 1915, E.T. Hazeltine died of a heart attack. Three years later, Dr. William Talbott also died, and Mary Fisher followed him in 1920. The company was suddenly bereft of its leaders and on the decline. In 1947, chloroform was banned from use in tonics, and consumption, though still in existence, was largely under control by the official medical establishment. Quack doctors and remedies were no longer in demand.

Finally, in 1951, the company and its assets were sold by then-owner Henry R. Fisher. The cure that never really was had come to an end, leaving an era of rural concocted medicine in the past while emerging into a world of mass-produced pharmaceuticals with sometimes similarly questionable claims. Piso's Cure for Consumption was just one tonic in a long line of panaceas that proclaimed an end to suffering for those damaged by pain.

RIDGWAY SANITARIUM AND ACME LINIMENT

For many good reasons, Northwestern Pennsylvania is often identified with oil—barrels and barges, fires and floods, robber barons and Rockefellers and even a criminal or two. Less often is considered all the things oil touched that were unrelated to moneymaking schemes or the greed that black gold inspired. For one man about seven miles away from the epicenter of the oil boom, oil was a catalyst for kindness and hope for the sick and weary.

Samuel Ridgway was born on April 29, 1824, the eighth of nine children, in what was then the wilderness of Crawford County, Pennsylvania. His father was Charles Ridgway and his mother Frances Titus Ridgway, the sister of Jonathan Titus, the founder of Titusville. As a boy, Samuel played with his siblings and the few other children who lived in the sparsely populated, difficult-to-access woodland area known as Oil Creek. The first commercial oil well had not yet been drilled, and there were no millionaires at the site when Samuel was a young man in Northwestern Pennsylvania.

In 1848, Ridgway married Eliza Hyde, and the couple had eight children: Frances, Diademma, Ida, Eliza, Samuel E., Willis, Charles and Mallie. Shortly after his thirty-fifth birthday, Samuel's whole world changed when Edwin Drake struck oil and people poured into his corner of the county by the thousands. In Oil Creek, now called Hydetown, the population increased as the Titusville citizenry swelled and spread, capitalizing on the boomtown atmosphere.

THE PHILLIPS AND WOODFORD WELLS. TARR FARM.

Early oil field photo near the Tarr Farm in Titusville, Pennsylvania. *Photo by John Mather, 1861.*

At the time, infrastructure was improving so that oil could be transported out of town and into the hands of buyers. Ridgway seized an opportunity and became a purchasing agent with the Oil Creek Railroad. He was well known in the area for his big heart and magnanimous personality. Unsatisfied with his railroad job, he began experimenting with crude oil as medicine. At first, the benzine-based substance was used to cure cattle ills, but to his surprise, people began requesting his treatments for personal use.

In order to treat patients, in 1882 he built the Ridgway Sanitarium in Hydetown, which acted as a hospital and health retreat for the afflicted. On July 3, 1883, he was granted a patent from the United States Patent Office (no. 3341) for Ridgway Acme Liniment. Ridgway's liniment was intended to be used medicinally for the relief and even purported cure of rheumatism, neuralgia, cancers and more.

Ridgway Sanitarium was located on the main railway line, and patients clamored for a chance to be treated by Ridgway, with his special liniment and massage technique that were said to heal them of almost any ailment. The sign on the building read, "The Last Resort for Suffering Humanity," and for many it was their salvation. Unfortunately for Ridgway, while he was healing the wounds of a suffering humanity, he was also suffering personal tragedy.

The Ridgway family was a very tight-knit group, and they all raised their families together and communed with one another often. In 1890, the large family was dealt two significant blows without any recovery time in between. On June 18, 1890, Ridgway's daughter Ida died suddenly at only thirty-six years old. While the family was occupied grieving the loss of their sister and daughter, they could not see the next tragedy they were about to endure. Just one week later, Diademma "Demma" Ridgway Aikin died on June 27 at the young age of thirty-nine. Demma was married to Charles Aikin and had four children, two of whom survived childhood (Edna and Homer) and two of whom died young (Frances at age nineteen and Anna at age three). In the span of a few short days, the Ridgway family lost two of their closest members and the heartbeat of the family. Arrested by their grief, the Ridgways had to figure out how to endure and took comfort in healing people with their father's invention.

Ridgway Sanitarium and Ridgway Acme Liniment were advertised far and wide across not only the region but also the state and the nation. In 1892, the *Wellsville Allegany County Democrat*, located in New York, reported, "The Ridgway Sanitarium is fast making a reputation" and that "the cures there perfected are something marvelous." In 1899, the *Smethport McKean Democrat* advertised the liniment for sale at the local drugstore. Residents of towns all over Pennsylvania and surrounding states gushed about their positive experiences at the sanitarium and encouraged others to seek treatment there. Mentions of patients treated and cured appeared in newspapers in Bradford, New Bethlehem, Smethport, Warren, Kinzua, Pineville and many other cities and towns. A few patients even traveled as far as Boston, Cleveland and Canada for Ridgway's patented treatment. Due to Ridgway's fame, a liniment express order business was established, selling in drugstores across the country.

Ridgway Sanitarium housed as many as 150 patients at a time. This number is staggering compared to the full-time residency of only 300 citizens in Hydetown. Only two short years after coming to terms with the loss of two close family members, the Ridgways were hit yet again with heartbreak in 1892.

On May 3, 1892, around 4:30 p.m., a fire broke out in the sanitarium caused by an apparent lightning strike that ignited the oil-based liniment and turned the health resort into a towering inferno. A bucket brigade was immediately summoned, and people from the surrounding area raced to the scene to try to save their most famous business. The brigade found some success by stopping the fire from igniting the neighboring store and hotel but could not save the sanitarium itself. While the fire raged, seven people were inside the structure. Samuel Ridgway and his son, three patients and two young employees, Austie Bidwell and Cora Sabin, were trapped in the building. Young Ridgway and Cora Sabin escaped through a second-story window while the senior Ridgway helped all three patients to safety, including dragging a patient thrown to the floor by the blast out of the building. Both men were seriously burned about the hands and face.

The heat was intense. The flames were so wicked that the windows cracked in the storefront across the street from the sanitarium. As the fire was finally quelled, it was found that one person did not escape the building. Austie Bidwell, only seventeen years old, was found charred in the remains of the laboratory. The *Titusville Herald* reported that Bidwell was "in the packing room, where the flames started. She was enveloped in a sheet of fire, and probably death was almost instantaneous from inhalation of the flames."

Austie was a close friend of the Ridgways and had lived with them ever since her mother died the previous year. They were extremely distraught by her death, and Samuel Ridgway paid for her funeral, including what was described as an "elegant casket." She was buried beside her mother, Calista White Bidwell, at Lyona Cemetery in Centerville. The sanitarium only carried $600 in insurance, but the family was determined to rebuild. Before they could begin, Austie's estranged father, Oscar Bidwell, tried to extort $3,000 from Samuel Ridgway for his daughter's death. When Ridgway refused to comply, Oscar had Samuel arrested. Fortunately, the court saw through the farce and threw the case out a few months later, stating, "The matter is looked upon here as a very foolish attempt to extort a little money out of Uncle Sam, and that perhaps other parties besides Bidwell are mourning less interested in the swag."

Despite the 1892 fire, the rebuilt sanitarium and liniment continued to grow in popularity. Samuel Ridgway died on April 9, 1901, of diabetes at home after enjoying many years of prosperity in his self-made businesses. He is buried at Ridgway Cemetery, his family namesake, in Hydetown. Upon his death, the business was run by his daughter, Eliza Ridgway Nason. Unlike most entrepreneurial family businesses, instead of passing the sanitarium and liniment on to one of his sons, Ridgway bequeathed the business to his daughter. Along with her husband, Sherman Ellsworth Nason, Eliza ran the business for two years until leasing it to a Mr. Heaston and Mr. Anderson of Cleveland. This would turn out to be a costly and terrible decision.

On September 29, 1903, at 2:00 p.m., the sanitarium caught fire again, this time leveling the building. As telegraph operator Smith and funeral director McNett were walking by the business, they noticed smoke and looked aghast at the roof of the sanitarium. A bucket brigade was once again assembled, but the key to the fire hydrant was broken and the fire quickly spread. The Titusville Fire Department Colonel Drake Steamer, driven by a team of horses, raced to the scene. They were unable to save the structure, as the fire had already raged for a half an hour and the water pressure was too weak to make much of a difference. As the roof caved in, people watched astounded as their local hero's life's work was once again consumed by flame.

Thankfully, though thirty patients were in the sanitarium at the time of the blaze, all escaped without injury. Although the insurance had been increased from the previous fire, it was still not enough to cover the more than $15,000 worth of damage and destruction. Unlike the 1892 fire, the second fire was of an undetermined cause since the part of the building that caught fire had no electricity or pipes. It was theorized that it could have been caused by a spark thrown by a passing train on the nearby railroad. Nason and her husband rebuilt the sanitarium from their own money and operated it as the proprietors for another seven years.

Like the original sanitarium, the twice-rebuilt version included a grand office, a smoking room, a sitting room, a parlor, multiple apartments and a kitchen on the first floor. The second story featured eighteen guest rooms. The structure was heated by steam and lit by gas. It had its own sewage system and separate cottages for extra patients. By the time it opened again in December 1903, it was already completely booked.

The last patient treated at the sanitarium was released in 1910, and the business was put up for sale in July 1911. The second iteration of the Ridgway Sanitarium still stands today as the Rustic Inn, and Ridgway's family still resides in Hydetown. Samuel Ridgway's sanitarium and acme liniment grew to nationwide fame, as did its ingenuous and kindhearted proprietor. Ridgway never expected payment from his patients, always treating them due to a compulsion to ease human suffering. Samuel Ridgway and his family are some of the few pioneers of Northwestern Pennsylvania who predate the oil boom. Samuel Ridgway's entrepreneurial spirit and caring heart, and the hard work of his family in the face of immense tragedy and heartbreak, put Hydetown on the map, not just for Northwestern Pennsylvanians but in the mind of the nation.

THE OREGON INDIAN MEDICINE COMPANY

In this rural corner of Pennsylvania, medicine and doctors were few and far between. Hardy pioneers and their descendants had to rely on traditions, folkways and even traveling bands of purported professionals for supplies and information. Medicine shows featuring a mix of entertainment and resources traveled throughout the United States peddling wares to the needy people of isolated towns across the landscape. One of the most famous of those companies set up shop in Corry, Pennsylvania, in the late nineteenth century.

The Oregon Indian Medicine Company was founded by Colonel Thomas Augustus Edwards in Pittsburgh, Pennsylvania, in 1876. Edwards was born in 1832 in New York. He worked as a circus manager and traveled across the still-wild West, racking up legions of adventures along the way. It was even purported that Edwards served as a spy during the Civil War.

During his adventures in the West, Edwards met the man who would become his business partner. Donald McKay, born 1836 in Oregon, was half-Cayuse Native American and half-Scottish. In 1852, at the young age of sixteen, McKay began working for the United States Army and Bureau of Indian Affairs. When the Modoc War broke out in 1872, he served as captain of the Warm Springs Indian Scouts and played an integral role in trying to negotiate between the two sides.

The Modoc War was between the Native American Modoc people in Northern California and Southern Oregon and the United States. The Modoc were incensed by colonial incursion into their land and struck out against a small band of explorers. In retribution, the explorers attacked a Klamath Native American village that had nothing to do with the ambush, destroying their structures and killing warriors, women and children. In an effort to end hostilities, negotiations went back and forth for years. Both sides were unsuccessful, and violence increased.

Donald McKay attempted to help the two sides reach a peace agreement by negotiating with Kintpuash, also known as Captain Jack, leader of the Modoc Tribe. The negotiations stalled, and many more people on both sides died as a result. Eventually, the Modocs were defeated. Kintpuash and three of his lead warriors were captured and executed, two lead warriors were sentenced to life imprisonment in Alcatraz and the Modoc people, including the wives and children of the executed warriors, were expelled from their land and sent to the Quapaw Territory in Oklahoma, 1,800 miles from home.

Photograph of the Warm Springs Scouts in the Lava Beds of California, with leader and future Oregon Indian Medicine Company employee Donald McKay in center. *U.S. National Archives and Records Administration at College Park, 1873.*

After the war, McKay tried his hand at starring in Wild West shows to survive. In the autumn of 1876, he met Edwards and decided to pair up to help sell Edwards's products. McKay; his wife, Tuuepum; daughter, Minnie; and brother, Dr. William C. McKay, who would help with production and marketing, packed up their lives and made their way east.

The two most famous traveling Indian medicine shows were the Kickapoo Indian Medicine Company, which had no relation to the Kickapoo Nation, and the Oregon Indian Medicine Company. The shows traveled with various

Portrait of Donald McKay, chief of the Warm Springs Indians and future traveling medicine showman. *Denver Library Digital Collections, Thomas Houseworth, circa 1880.*

entertainment acts and pitchmen, who were usually white people posing as Native Americans, to sell their "medicinal elixirs." These shows could range anywhere from a single horse and wagon show to huge tents employing dozens of people and acts.

Usually, stages were constructed of a raised platform with a canvas awning. Sometimes, a three-sided canvas enclosed the stage, providing a more dramatic backdrop for the acts and the medicinal pitches. Fancier shows traveled with a large curtain in the front and were lit with gasoline torches. Seating for the audience was rustic, being constructed of planks of wood placed on top of soap boxes. When these seats were all taken, people would continue to crowd in until the ground was covered with people standing and sitting in every open space. People clamored from miles around to take in the excitement that an Oregon Indian Medicine Company show delivered.

After keeping their headquarters in Pittsburgh and traveling for six years, Edwards and McKay decided to move the company to Corry in 1882 to take advantage of the railroad and central location of a booming rural population. The show was popular, featuring drama, vaudeville, comedy, music, burlesque and more. Between acts, pitchmen took the stage to hawk

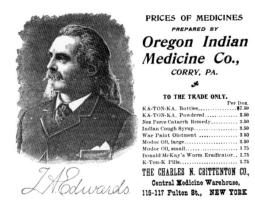

PRICES OF MEDICINES
PREPARED BY

Oregon Indian Medicine Co.,

CORRY, PA.

TO THE TRADE ONLY.

	Per Doz.
KA-TON-KA, Bottles,	$7.50
KA-TON-KA, Powdered	3.50
Nez Perce Catarrh Remedy	3.50
Indian Cough Syrup	3.50
War Paint Ointment	3.50
Modoc Oil, large	3.50
Modoc Oil, small	1.75
Donald McKay's Worm Eradicator	1.75
K-Ton-K Pills	1.75

THE CHARLES N. CRITTENTON CO.,

Central Medicine Warehouse,

115-117 Fulton St., NEW YORK

Oregon Indian Medicine Company advertisement. *From Proprietary Medicines and Druggists Sundries Catalogue, 1902–3, page 324.*

over-the-counter medications with appropriated or fake tribal names. The Oregon company's most popular elixirs were Ka-Ton-Ka, Nez Perce Catarrh Snuff and War Paint Ointment.

In this era, the belief ran rampant that the land held a natural cure for all diseases that infected the people in that area and that native peoples were most acquainted with those cures. Theater historian Brooks McNamara analyzed these traveling medicine shows and described how "[m]any white Americans believed that the Indian was a natural physician, endowed with an iron constitution because he possessed secrets of healing unknown to the white man." Native Americans were looked on as symbols of strength and purity, even while the American government was simultaneously forcing them from their ancestral homes.

Quack doctors used the reputation of Native Americans and their true natural medicines to capitalize on public sentiment and make a profit. Native American culture and knowledge was used as an exhibition and an entertainment act for which one could buy a ticket and maybe even the secret to health. "By the nineteenth century," McNamara explained, "Indian performers were often reduced to dime museum novelties whose songs and dances had become the delight of rubberneck tourists."

The Oregon Indian Medicine Company toured across Northwestern Pennsylvania and southern New York, attracting crowds and selling thousands of bottles of elixir. In 1888, the *Warren Mirror* reported that while the company was performing in Wellsville, New York, a young woman fell in love with a performer. When the show left town, she followed and was spurned by the entertainer. In an act of fatal revenge, the young woman, called Miss Scott, swallowed poison and died, spurring the headline "Woman Suicides for Love of a Dashing Showman."

All the elixirs sold in Corry were purportedly made on the Umatilla Reservation in Oregon, where Donald McKay had local connections. McKay and his family worked for Edwards in Northwestern Pennsylvania for ten years before moving home to the Umatilla Reservation, where he lived until his death in 1899. Edwards held McKay in such high reverence that he even published a biography of his life in 1884.

At the turn of the century, the company began declining in popularity. In 1916, it took an enormous hit when the United States Bureau of Chemistry targeted its elixirs for testing. The bureau decided to test the bestselling product, Ka-Ton-Ka, under the Pure Food and Drug Act. It found that the medicine was merely a combination of alcohol, sugar, aloes and baking soda. The bureau fined the company, declaring that the purported medicine was "misbranded for the reason that certain statements appearing on its labels falsely and fraudulently represented it as effected as a blood medicine in the treatment of all kidney and liver complaints, erysipelas [similar to cellulitis], female troubles, fever and ague, rheumatism, dyspepsia, catarrh [a mucus-filled cough], scrofula [from tuberculosis], blood poison, syphilis, and malaria, and as a remedy for all blood diseases, salt rheum, enlargement of the liver, and diseases of the kidneys, when, in truth and in fact, it was not."

The Oregon Indian Medicine Company pleaded no contest to the charge by the Bureau of Chemistry and paid the $200 fine levied by the Department of Agriculture. This charge was the beginning of the end of fake medicine peddled under Native American names. The availability of scientific medicine was growing, and medical doctors were more common in rural areas where they could treat needy patients more regularly.

When it came to medical care in the frontier of Northwestern Pennsylvania, the ratio of institutionally trained medical professionals to patients in need was astronomically high. Concoctions, clinics and even traveling shows provided a semblance of care for the booming and medically neglected population so susceptible to injury and death. Residents of these far-flung areas connected only by railroads, if they were lucky, clamored to take advantage of cures for their ailments and relief from suffering. Not all the elixirs peddled to the populace were honest. Medical doctors probably shook their heads at the crowds who spent their hard-earned dollars on shows and placebos. Rural medicine was rough and raw in the early stages of the region's development, and people did the best they could to survive, whether that meant being the consumers or inventors of questionable cures. Sometimes even a placebo could be enough to soothe the injuries inflicted by frontier life in Northwestern Pennsylvania.

CHAPTER 7

HURRICANES OF POWER

Mothers, Daughters and Granddaughters in NWPA

CAROLINE ELDRED WATSON AND ANNA WATSON SYMS

When author and poet Maya Angelou was asked to describe her mother, she spoke of her as a hurricane in its perfect power. Men are used to power, to being in charge. When women recognize their power and act on it to change the world, they are truly immeasurable, using all their force to whip up a fury of change that leaves something wholly different in its wake. Caroline Eldred Watson and her daughter, Anna Watson Syms, took the power endowed on them by the grace of great wealth and used it to better their family, friends and their Warren County community with very little recognition. But recognition was never part of their plan.

Caroline Eldred Watson was born on April 20, 1836, in Warren, Pennsylvania, the daughter of Nathaniel Bailey Eldred and Sarah Melissa Dimmick. Nathaniel Eldred was a successful lawyer. He rose through the ranks of his profession and gained great acclaim as a just man of the law. Nathaniel was proud of his career, and in all the writings about him, there is hardly any mention his parents, wife or slew of children who were most certainly running about the house. When Caroline was only three years old, her father was appointed president judge of the Sixth District Court of Pennsylvania, which included Erie, Crawford and Venango Counties. Coming from a high-powered and esteemed family,

Caroline's future was preordained. She was to marry well and continue the prestigious family heritage.

On June 18, 1856, she became the second wife of another reputable Northwestern Pennsylvanian, Colonel Lewis Findlay Watson. Watson had been previously married, and his first wife passed away. Sixteen years her senior, Watson was born in Titusville on April 14, 1819, and moved to Warren the year Caroline was born. He was an industrious young man and made his mark as a merchant and banker, eventually founding the Conewango Valley Railroad Company and becoming the president of Warren Savings Bank in 1870. He was elected to the United States House of Representatives three times as a Republican, serving intermittently between 1877 and his death in 1890. The Watson family was popular and wealthy, but Caroline, as the dutiful congressional wife, was always in the shadows.

Through her parentage and her marriage, Caroline Eldred Watson accrued a large sum of money. Although she was well-off financially, she endured great emotional hardship. In 1868, her son, Nathaniel Eldred Watson, died at only ten years old. The couple also had a daughter, Anna, born on December 19, 1860, who survived to adulthood—their only living child. In 1890, her husband died, leaving Caroline a widow at only fifty-four years old.

Despite the obvious sadness that plagued her after the death of her son and husband, Caroline Eldred Watson was not a woman with time to waste. She quickly began to use her free time to expand her mind and see the world. She traveled often to Philadelphia, where her daughter lived, spent time with friends and even sailed abroad to Europe with her best friend, Anna Oaks. A devoted member of the Presbyterian Church, she was prominent in social activities and was known as a generous and kind socialite in Warren.

Caroline spread her zest for life and caring for her community to her only child, Anna. Another Watson woman who led a difficult life and persevered, Anna Watson Syms's early life was full of undisclosed pain. Not only did she lose her brother in childhood, but Anna also endured a life "which almost from her girlhood was one of pain and suffering, with limited periods of comparative comfort. Whilst of necessity deprived of the opportunity of entering into the activities of life, she retained a keen interest in affairs and utilized her enforced confinement in study and in plans for the advancement of the interests of others."

After her marriage to Parker Syms, Anna moved to Coronado, California, where she created a beautiful house for her mother and extended family to enjoy while she lived the rest of the year in Philadelphia. She was widowed

Image of the business district in Warren, Pennsylvania, between 1930 and 1945. *Boston Public Library, Tichnor Brothers Collection, no. 79830.*

early in life, with Parker dying sometime before 1905. Despite moving away, Anna never forgot her home. She was called "Lady Bountiful" by the people of Warren and was said to respond to "all appeals of a charitable or public nature. An evidence of her interest in her native town is the beautiful chancel of Trinity Church donated by her when the present church was erected as a memorial to her father, for many years a member of this vestry."

Anna and Caroline lived in her Coronado house for the betterment of their health for many months out of the year. As Anna's health began to decline, she became incapable of doing everyday tasks and traveled to University Hospital in Philadelphia for one last attempt at recovery. After undergoing two unspecified operations, Anna contracted pneumonia. Immediately, her mother and her niece, as well as her adopted daughter, Mary Hamlin Lucy, rushed to her side. Anna died on December 2, 1917. She was fifty-six years old.

Even in death, Anna was not done giving. In her will, she gave $25,000 to the University of Pennsylvania John Herr Musser Medical Research Laboratory; a house in Warren to her cousin Arthur Gordon Eldred; $30,000 to her friend Helen Mary Durfee, with an additional $1,200 annual salary; and her California home, "Manna," to her adopted daughter, Mary, whom she adored.

Caroline Eldred Watson was crushed by the death of her only child. Suddenly, on January 6, 1919, Caroline died, shocking the entire Warren

1910 census record showing Anna Watson Syms living with her mother, Caroline Watson, in Warren, Pennsylvania. *U.S. Census Bureau.*

community. She was in very good health, and no one, including her family, expected her sudden demise. At her death, Caroline requested a private ceremony with no flowers, not wanting anything to go to waste. She knew that she was extremely blessed in life, despite her trials, and was determined not to be ostentatious in death. Unfortunately, her death did not receive much coverage in the local newspaper, as she died the same day as former president Theodore Roosevelt. While his name was splashed across the front page and mourners wept their outpourings of grief, Caroline Eldred Watson's life languished in the back of the newspaper, forgotten by many. But she did not forget them.

In her last will and testament, Caroline had a plan that would forever affect the Warren community and the women who lived there. With the fortune she protected throughout her life, upon her death she bequeathed more than $1 million for the creation of a home for older women where they could live out their natural lives in peace and serenity. The home was called the Watson Memorial Home, and her will specified that it be a home for "indigent women of sixty-five years or older and without a spouse," either widowed, unmarried or divorced. She also stipulated that the women accepted must *want* to live there, as she did not want family members forcing their aged relatives out of their homes. Her home was a place of refuge for the souls of weary women across the area who needed a place of rest with nowhere else to turn. For many, Caroline Eldred Watson was a saving grace.

The Watson Memorial Home was opened on July 8, 1935. It included four parlors and a reading room in addition to the many residential rooms. It was truly a home away from home. Watson's intention was for $30,000 of the more than $1 million to be used directly for the building of the home and the rest for continual support over time. The home, still open and serving women to this day, has no minimum financial requirement for its residents. Once a woman's assets have been exhausted, or if she enters with none, the Watson Home continues her care. Single women in

Lush landscape view of Warren, Pennsylvania, from Washington Park, showing the mix of city life and beautiful scenery such as that the Watsons would have experienced. *Boston Public Library, Tichnor Brothers Collection, no. 78355.*

need were not and are not turned away in the spirit of Caroline's selfless gift. The Watson women both turned their struggles into triumphs and used their blessings to better their communities immeasurably. Their power can still be felt today.

Emma Lawrence and Ada Louise Lawrence

Being a woman is hard. In the nineteenth century, it was even harder. To add to that hardship, include the additional layer of being African American in a majority white city before the Civil War. That is the world into which Emma Gertrude Lawrence was born in the late 1850s.

Lawrence was born an orphan on April 18, 1858, in Ohio. Her mother was African American and her father Native American. At the time of her birth, the Civil War had not yet even begun, and there were still nearly 4 million enslaved people and only about 250,000 free African Americans in the United States. The world into which Emma Gertrude Lawrence was born was not a world in which her skin color and her free status were particularly welcome. Without many options and in an attempt to make a

1910 census record showing a widowed Emma Lawrence and her four children after she started her business. *U.S. Census Bureau.*

better life for herself, Emma ran away from her foster parents in Buffalo and ended up in Erie, Pennsylvania.

After living in Erie for a while, Emma met John Lawrence. The couple started a family and began raising their three sons, Earl, Charley and Ray, and one daughter, Effie. Emma's life took another harsh blow in 1889 when John died suddenly.

At the young age of thirty, Emma Lawrence suddenly had to figure out how to raise four children alone. In 1890, only 30 black women in the entire *nation* held baccalaureate degrees (compared to 2,500 white women). African American women, particularly those widowed or divorced, were already a large part of the labor force by 1890, but they mostly took jobs in unskilled work. Life for African Americans in Erie was taking shape but continued to be influenced by external forces like hostility and racism, internal forces such as community culture and religion and structural forces like housing and transportation. The majority of jobs available to African American women were as piecemeal laundresses, servants, cooks or seamstresses. Because of prejudice, systemic racial issues, lack of opportunity and an expectation of domesticity, African American women filled roles that no one else wanted to fill. But Emma Lawrence was not willing to back down from a challenge.

Like many African American women, both married and single, who needed to support themselves or their children, Emma Lawrence began taking in other people's laundry piece by piece to make money. As the pieces stacked up and people gave Emma rave reviews on her service, she knew that she had a potential business opportunity on her hands. After years of making ends meet and raising her children as a laundress, she struck out on her own as a business owner and founded her own dry cleaning and dyeing company in 1906.

Lawrence Dyeing and Cleaning was located on Third and Chestnut Streets in Erie, Pennsylvania, and became a hub of African American life and culture in the city. Emma was the first African American woman in the city of Erie to own her own business. By 1916, her business had become lucrative enough to afford official advertisement in the city directory.

Emma Lawrence was said to have a "quiet force that commanded respect." She had raised four children, overcome adversity and made history all before her fiftieth birthday. She was a force to be reckoned with. She was known all across town for her special talent in working with dyes and colors. All of the work that needing dyeing or coloring went specifically to her for her expertise and skill. In the span of a single lifetime, she moved the needle by which African American women were measured by creating, learning and becoming a highly skilled entrepreneur and business proprietor.

Two of Emma's sons went on to become musicians. Ray Lawrence was a pianist and orchestra leader, and Earl was a music teacher. Emma Gertrude Lawrence died on May 10, 1934, at age seventy-five. Her family continued to operate the Lawrence Dyeing and Cleaning Business on Third and Chestnut until 1963, growing her legacy as one of the greatest women in Erie County history. She was not the only Lawrence to earn that title.

Music teacher Earl Lawrence, son of Emma Gertrude Lawrence and John Lawrence, married Belle Clark, and their daughter became one of the best-known history-making women of Erie: Ada Louise Lawrence. Ada was born on October 21, 1920, in Erie. She graduated from Strong Vincent High School in 1939 and enrolled at Cheyney State Teachers College (now Cheyney University) near Philadelphia, more than four hundred miles from home.

Ada was called to be a teacher and was determined to change the lives of young people in Erie. After graduating from Cheyney with a bachelor's degree in elementary education, Lawrence returned to Erie and applied to be a teacher in the Erie Public School System. School segregation had been outlawed in Pennsylvania since 1881, when Meadville resident Elias Allen refused to send his son to a segregated all-black school and sued the county. Crawford County judge Pearson Church ruled that the law

1930 census record showing Ada Louise Lawrence as a child living with her parents in the city of Erie. *U.S. Census Bureau.*

segregating schools by race was unconstitutional, and the Pennsylvania legislature agreed, passing a law officially outlawing segregation in public spaces in 1887. However, the law was not always followed, and de facto segregation was widespread. School districts were partitioned to ensure the separation of children of different races, and because of community shape and demographics, de facto segregation continues in districts across the nation to this day.

In the 1940s, Ada Louise Lawrence knew the fight she was up against when she made her intentions known of being an educator of black *and* white children enrolled in public school in the city of Erie. Several white parents expressed dismay at the thought of Lawrence teaching their children. Due to Erie's relative isolation from areas with larger African American populations, changes in societal attitude toward minorities evolved very slowly. Author Sarah S. Thompson noted, "Although the institution of slavery and those elderly reminders of its legacy were fading from sight, it remained a part of the community's collective consciousness." During Emma Lawrence's time, there were only about 300 African Americans in Erie, whereas by the time Ada Louise Lawrence was ready to fight for her right to teach, the black population had grown to almost 1,400 people.

Ada teamed up with her father to make her case as to why she was an ideal educator to hire. Earl was a well-respected and widely known figure in the community, and he sent a legion of letters to the mayor and city officials supporting his daughter and explaining how students needed an African American teacher to serve as an example of the potential and purpose their lives innately held. Ada Louise was not only intelligent, educated and incredibly qualified, he argued, but she would also serve as a necessary role model for black and white students alike. Earl and Ada won the fight, and her obituary stated that she was hired as the first black teacher in the Erie Public School System.

Eventually, Lawrence went back to school and graduated from Gannon University with a master's degree in guidance and counseling. In addition to her life as a teacher, she was also devoted to her church at the Episcopal Cathedral of St. Paul, helped create the Martin Luther King Jr. Center, served on the board of directors of the Dr. Gertrude Barber Center and was active in the local branch of the NAACP and the Harry T. Burleigh Society.

Lawrence looked up to and grew up knowing Harry T. Burleigh, whose family lived in the same neighborhood as the Lawrences near the bayfront. Burleigh was a famous African American composer and baritone singer born in Erie in 1866. Like Ada, Harry Burleigh's mother, Elizabeth, possessed a college degree and worked as a teacher in Erie. Elizabeth applied to be a teacher in the Erie Public School System but was denied and taught elsewhere, making Ada's breaking of the color barrier years later all the sweeter for her family and friends.

Ada Louise Lawrence was a woman of many interests and was known for her love of traveling and bowling, skill on the viola, adoration of her cats and intense passion for history and knowledge. She dedicated her later life to collecting the history of the African American community in Erie and making it known. In 2013, the street she and her family lived on was renamed Lawrence Family Way by the City of Erie.

Ada Louise Lawrence died on March 6, 2014, at the age of ninety-three. Continuing her grandmother's legacy of intelligence, skill, perseverance and love, Ada lived a hard-fought, historic life. Emma Gertrude Lawrence was dealt one of the most difficult hands one could hold in the nineteenth century as an orphaned, widowed African American mother of four. She did everything she could to provide for her family while achieving a dream of something more. The Lawrence family boasts the first African American woman business owner and first African American public school teacher in Erie history. The Lawrence women were forces to be reckoned with, shattering ceilings and inspiring countless people in Erie County for more than one hundred years.

CHARLOTTE WEBSTER BATTLES AND CHARLOTTE ELIZABETH BATTLES

The Battles family of Girard were a family of titans. Some people are familiar with the story of Asa Battles Sr. and his family lineage in the Erie County canal town. Far fewer know the role of the powerful Battles women, the two Charlottes, who took Northwestern Pennsylvania business and capitalism by storm.

Before either Charlotte yet existed, Asa Battles Sr. was already cementing the Battles name as a cultural and business leader in Girard. Born in 1786 in New York, Asa moved to Girard with his wife, Elizabeth Brown, in 1824. The couple had four children, the youngest of whom, born in 1833, was Rush S. Battles, who would inherit his parents' estate.

The Battleses were successful farmers, usually of fruit. Rush Battles inherited the farm his father so carefully cultivated with potatoes, corn,

Early photo of a horse and cart on a main road in Girard, Pennsylvania, by J.S. Leedham. *New York Public Library.*

wheat, barley and wide sweeping orchards of fruit and nut trees. The Battles Fruit Farm produced acres upon acres of fruit, including their much sought-after grapes, each year.

On March 28, 1861, Rush married Charlotte McConnell Webster, the daughter of a prominent mercantilist in the community. In addition to running the farm, Rush Battles earned a degree from the National Law School and cofounded the Battles and Webster House of Banking in Girard with his brother-in-law, Henry Webster. Battles used his good fortune to further invest in multiple communities in Northwestern Pennsylvania. He was the secretary-treasurer of the Girard Wrench Factory, one of the largest employers in the area. He also purchased the Climax Manufacturing Company of Corry at sheriff's sale and converted it to geared locomotive manufacturing in 1883. Through his leadership, the company produced one thousand locomotives from 1888 to 1928, making it one of the key industries in Erie County. Despite all his industrial success, Rush Battles's heart was always in farming.

Continuing his father's love of fruit cultivation, Battles produced Concord, Catawba, Isabella, Iona and Hartford Prolific grapes at the Pleasant View Farm. He increased the production of the farm even further, including apples, pears, peaches, cherries, plums, horse chestnuts, black walnuts and rare ornamentals such as Paulownias of China. This hard work by the Battles family became extremely important to their future when Rush Battles died on March 27, 1904, at the age of seventy. Suddenly, his wife, Charlotte Webster Battles, had to nurture the legacy created by the Battles name for the past hundred years. She was more than ready to step into her role.

Charlotte McConnell Webster Battles was born in 1835, a native of Girard. She was a very educated woman, studying in both Pennsylvania and New York. She was incredibly progressive and deeply invested in using her prominence to better the status of others, especially in her most loved realm, education. She was an active traveler, a devoted member of the Presbyterian Church and a gifted choir member. Upon the death of her husband, Charlotte Webster Battles knew that her life had to change from socialite to businesswoman and took charge of the family's investments and businesses. Like most women of her time, she endured her share of hardships. As a young wife, she and Rush wanted to start a family, but their first two children died in infancy. Finally, their daughter, Charlotte Elizabeth Battles, the namesake of her mother, survived and became the apple of her parents' eye. Yet Charlotte Elizabeth was not a delicate doll to be protected. She, too, was a force to be reckoned with.

Born on October 11, 1864, Charlotte Elizabeth Battles, called "Libbie" by her close friends, knew that she had large shoes to fill as a woman in the 1800s who would eventually inherit a great deal of wealth, property and prestige. Even as a young woman with a great deal of weight on her shoulders, she was not immune to a youthful indiscretion—one that almost ravaged her reputation.

Much to the shock of the community, Libbie suddenly married a virtual stranger, Charles E. Barber, a Washington, D.C., lawyer, in 1886 at twenty-two years old. Where once she was a free-spirited youngster, an only child in a prominent family who was adored by the community, she was swept up in the glamour of life in Washington, D.C., as the wife of a rising-star lawyer. The marriage was less than perfect. Libbie's cousin Rebecca McConnell Rice wrote letters in which she referred to a "beastly attack" on Libbie by her husband, Charles, and noted that the marriage was falling apart. Rebecca went on to say that "his charges are distorted villainous stories.…If money was his object in marrying Libbie I am sure he would have fared better by treating her well."

Abused and downtrodden, Libbie returned to Girard in the summer of 1887 with modest hopes of being accepted back into the community that

Stereoscopic photo of Main Street in Girard, where the Battles women would have strolled, by J.S. Leedham. *New York Public Library.*

loved her when her husband did not. Thankfully, Girard welcomed her with open arms, and although people talked about what must have happened between the two, whether it be attempts at extortion or physical abuse, she quickly became a central figure in the community once again.

Before her father's passing, Libbie encouraged him to build a new bank in 1893, made from state-of-the-art fireproof materials and an object of envy to all other banks. He heeded her advice and constructed a bank with walls twenty-four inches thick and a nearly impenetrable vault of thirty-six-inch-thick material. After her father's death, something almost equally as shocking happened: Libbie became the president of the R.S. Battles Bank and took over the family farm. She leased the old Battles home to tenant farmers. The tenants' families lived on the estate, and many children were born and raised there. At only forty years old, divorced and at the dawn of a new century, Libbie Battles was writing her name down permanently as a titan of business in Northwestern Pennsylvania.

Using her business acumen and soaring reputation, Libbie Battles was made a member of the Girard School Board and campaigned actively for worthy expenditures, such as making the schools an engaging place to learn for Girard youth. Not to be outdone in the realm of education, Charlotte Webster Battles donated $20,000 to the creation of a new school building in 1910 to rectify overcrowding and deplorable conditions at the Girard

Academy. After it was found that the $20,000 would not be enough to outfit the school, Charlotte, a "progressive, community minded, well educated woman," added another $15,000 and stipulated that the school must have regular maintenance and a four-acre playground for the children. She was so devoted to the project that she personally approved the bricks with which the school was constructed. They called it the Battles Memorial School.

The first graduating class of the new school processed in 1912, and the majority of its graduates were women. Charlotte and Libbie teamed up with Rush's sister, Lucina Battles, to create a library association in 1891. Lucina Battles had been collecting books as early as 1859, when books were hard to come by in rural areas, even for the wealthy. Charlotte and Libbie both served as officers of the library association, and Lucina was the head of book purchasing. A building was constructed in 1893 with money from Robertson Wilcox, and thus the Wilcox Library took shape as directed by the Battles women.

Charlotte and Libbie Battles—women who shared a name, a life and a legacy—were the best of friends. They spent almost every day together, shared their thoughts and loves and passions with each other and were truly each other's confidants. When her mother became ill and died in October 1920, Libbie was crushed. "A terrible loneliness overcame [her] after her mother's death," wrote Geoffrey Domowicz. "She had cousins in Girard, but there was no one to share her life with" anymore. In an instant, her whole world had shifted. With her mother and father both gone, she had to find a new purpose.

Around the same time, Libbie hired a young woman named Georgianna "Nan" Read to help care for the family, house and estate. Georgianna filled the void in Libbie's life left by the loss of her mother, and the two became fast, best friends. Together, they went shopping, to the opera and even traveled to California. They often entertained at the home they shared, playing bridge in the Ladies' Friday Bridge Club.

But fun and games were not enough to fulfill Libbie's passion and abilities. As the years wore on and the Great Depression began to affect rural Western Pennsylvania, Libbie was forced to face tough decisions as president of one of the biggest banks in the area. By 1933, there were runs on banks every day, with millions of dollars being withdrawn and crippling the economic foundation of the United States. To try to stem the hemorrhage, President Franklin Delano Roosevelt asked the governor of each state to place a moratorium on banking, and he proclaimed a cessation of all transactions from March 5 through March 9.

While Washington was panicking, Libbie Battles happened to be on vacation in California. Upon hearing the president's declaration, she immediately telegraphed her uncle, who was at the bank in Girard, and demanded that business continue as usual. There would be no moratorium at the R.S. Battles Bank. As the sole owner of the establishment, her demand was strictly enforced, and her bank was the *only* bank in the state of Pennsylvania to remain open—and one of very few in the entire country in defiance of the president's order.

On the Monday of the ignored moratorium, Libbie Battles almost dared the people of Girard to withdraw their money. Four farmers went and withdrew everything from their accounts (a hefty total sum of five dollars) but immediately put it all back. She was winning her standoff. Her bold decision even made it into the *New York Times* when on March 11, 1933, it ran a story about her defiance, stating that she was strong in her will that her bank was private and could not be controlled by the government. The federal government had no authority in Libbie Battles's bank, and she was ready to fight to make sure it stayed that way.

The leaders in Washington, D.C., were not happy with Libbie's unbowed stance. They ordered her to comply, and in response, she wrote a seething letter to the president that declared her unwillingness to budge. She wrote, "Mr. President, since I do not presume to tell you how to run the country, don't you presume to tell me how to run my bank. We're minding our business, you mind yours. C. Elizabeth Battles." The R.S. Battles Bank never did close throughout the crisis, and investors lost no money during Ms. Battles's standoff with the president of the United States.

In 1946, Libbie led the charge in merging the R.S. Battles Bank with the Girard National Bank, after which she retired from public life. After a lifetime of standing up for what she believed and living every second to its fullest, Charlotte Elizabeth Battles died on December 17, 1952, at the age of eighty-eight. In her obituary, the local newspaper mourned the loss of one of the town's greatest figures, calling her a "distinguished Girard citizen and philanthropist." In her life, Libbie Battles had been a business force in farming and banking, as well as finding time to serve her community on the school board, the library board, the garden club, the Daughters of the American Revolution, the Travelers Club and as cofounder of the Civic Improvement Association; she also became one of the first two women ever appointed to the board of trustees at the Edinboro Normal School in 1914.

After her death, Battles left her estate to her best friend, Georgianna Read, amounting to more than $3 million. Read used the money, as directed by

Battles, to create the Webster Home for the Aged in Libbie's grandparents' home. Georgianna lived in the house she shared with Libbie for thirty more years until her own death in 1982. After her passing, the Battles estate was bequeathed to the Erie County Historical Society, which now runs it as the Charlotte Elizabeth Battles Memorial Museum.

The Battles name goes back for many generations in Girard. The family created and sustained countless businesses and enterprises that supported the lives of scores of Northwestern Pennsylvanians throughout the years. Unsung in these exploits are the two Charlottes—Charlotte McConnell Webster Battles, the lover of education and gift to children, and Charlotte Elizabeth "Libbie" Battles, the woman who rose from the ashes of an abusive marriage to stand up to the president of the United States when she determined it necessary. The two Charlottes were not only strong women but also generous, savvy, intelligent, resilient, loving and distinguished. And just like the Northwestern Pennsylvanian women who came before and would come after them, they were hurricanes of power.

CHAPTER 8

Brawling Footballers, Black Baseball Pioneers and the Fastest Swayback Who Ever Lived

John Heisman: Tracing the Trophy to Titusville

Strolling down the dirt streets near the industrial center of East Titusville in the 1870s and '80s, you would have been greeted by dust and horses, metal clangs and hoofbeats and the hollers of a group of young boys playing a knock-down, drag-out game with no name. Out behind houses or in small fields, groups of young hellions would assemble after school to roll around in the dirt and mud chasing a ball, returning home with cut lips and bruised eyes. This mishmash of soccer and rugby would evolve into what we know today as American football and was played by youngsters all over the country. In Titusville, one young boy was a little more enamored of the sport than the rest. His name was John Heisman.

John Heisman was one of three boys born to German immigrants Michael and Sarah Lehr Heisman. Michael Heisman was born in Vorra, Germany, on January 1, 1835. His mother died when he was only twenty-one months old, claimed by dysentery. He was raised by his grandparents. Sarah Lehr was also born in Germany, in Bavaria.

A common misconception about the Heisman family name was promulgated through misinformation and folk rumor for decades. Many people, including Heisman family members, repeated the story that the Heisman family name actually came from Sarah Lehr's family because

Michael Heisman was the son of Baron Von Bogart, who disowned Michael when he announced his marriage to a peasant girl, Sarah Lehr. However, Heisman's great-nephew, upon hearing this oft-repeated rumor, wanted to confirm it officially and researched the family lineage. Not only did John M. Heisman, the great-nephew, find through birth, marriage and census records that this was not true, but he also discovered that the original family name was Heissmann and thus Michael's birth name was Johann Michael Heissmann. Michael was never disowned, nor did he take the surname of his wife. The story, like so many in immigrant families across the globe, was simply a casualty of the telephone game of family history.

Eventually, both Michael and Sarah immigrated separately to the United States in the 1850s. They both settled in Cleveland, where there were many German expatriates, and it was easy to create a small home away from home. The two finally met and were married in 1866. They immediately started their family with Daniel in 1867 and John in 1869. After living and working in Cleveland, the family caught wind of the oil boom in Pennsylvania and decided to migrate east.

First, the Heismans lived in Erie, where their third son, Michael, was born in 1872. Ready to capitalize on the oil fortunes being made in Titusville, the family moved there with their three young sons in 1874. Michael Heisman was a trained barrel cooper. His great-nephew, John M. Heisman, described how "shortly after Drake struck oil at his pioneer well [in 1859], wooden barrels became almost as valuable as the petroleum itself." Skilled labor in barrel cooperage was necessary since money could not be made until the oil arrived at market.

John Heisman grew up watching his father refine his skill in white oak and hickory by opening his own business, the Stephens & Heisman Cooper Shop. The success spurred Michael to invest in oil. In 1885, he became a partner in the American Oil Works, which created and owned the Penn Drake brand. This oil company was eventually bought out by Penreco in 1926, closing in 1948. Growing up during the oil boom in Titusville was important to the Heisman boys' formative years. "Titusville taught the Heisman boys lessons of life that each would take and build upon," wrote John M. Heisman, "personal responsibility; hard, persevering work; and honest dealings."

All three boys were educated at Titusville High School, and John played on the varsity football team as guard, was captain of the baseball team and was even a gymnast. He graduated in the class of 1887 as salutatorian and excelled as a student and public speaker. Although his father refused to watch his sons play the violent game of early football, the family was supportive of John's intellect and ability.

Just before John was to go off to school at Brown University, he got together with a few young men who were home from Princeton and the University of Pennsylvania for summer break. They told John about how football was played in college with rules, signals and a lack of punches, kicks and bites. John was both stunned and resistant to this new form of the game being played on the collegiate level. Upon arriving at Brown and trying out for the team, it was announced that the school had decided to drop the football program. John stayed at Brown for two years, but the enticement of playing football was simply too strong, and he transferred to the University of Pennsylvania before his junior year.

For the first time in his life, John Heisman was playing football that held some resemblance to the sport we avidly watch still today. He began guarding an oval ball, unlike the round, soccer-like ball of his youth. He was finally able to not only throw the ball but also carry it, running fast over the goal line. And on an even simpler note, he and his teammates now could wear uniforms, making it vastly simpler to tell who your teammate was.

One event that shaped the rest of Heisman's football life was when he accidentally broke a teammate's leg when making a tackle at full force.

The first team John Heisman coached at Oberlin College in 1892. *Oberlin College Archives, 1892.*

This accidental yet horrific injury became an obsession for Heisman. He industriously studied physics and the science of making an efficient yet safe tackle. He mastered the art and taught it to all players under his tutelage for the rest of his life. It would certainly be interesting to see what Heisman might think about the controversial tackling rules in today's National Football League.

On December 13, 1890, Heisman's life was forever changed by the sport he adored. Penn was playing Rutgers University at Madison Square Garden. While the players were practicing, the lights were being serviced. As Heisman ran by to catch a ball, the lights suddenly sprang on without notice, giving off a burst of light and noxious fumes that enveloped the twenty-one-year-old. His eyes stung, and he knew something was not right. He later found out that the fumes from the bulbs permanently damaged his eyes. Consequently, he could no longer read and began to struggle in school. The intellectual and dedicated Heisman refused to let the accident be the end of his career.

For his last year at Penn, Heisman teamed up with his friends to study together so that he would not fall behind. When it came time for his final exams, with an eloquent speech he convinced his professors to allow him to take his exams orally. They conceded, and he passed with flying colors. John Heisman graduated from Penn in 1892 with a baccalaureate degree in law but knew that he could no longer study the written law or play the game he loved. He was forced to chart a new path.

Immediately after graduation, Heisman knew that if he could not study the law or play football, he would become a coach and joined the staff of an infant program at Oberlin College. Given his many personal obstacles in life, including his small stature, he was a staunch supporter of letting anyone who wished to try out the chance to play. He believed that size was not a determinant of success, and he helped mold the rules so that everyone had a part to play. Furthermore, he was dead set that his players perform well in school or else they could not be on the field. He often repeated to his players that the body's greatness meant nothing with an uneducated mind. He knew that football did not last forever and wanted more than fame and glory for his young men.

In his early coaching career, Heisman moved around often. He left Oberlin after one year, moving to Buchtel College. He continued his tour of college coaching at Auburn and Clemson, eventually landing at the school that would deliver him greatness. At Georgia Tech, Heisman made his home from 1904 to 1919, coaching football, baseball and basketball. Although it took many seasons of stops and starts, he eventually led Georgia Tech

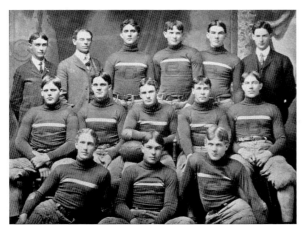

Above: Photograph taken at a meeting of the Auburn University and University of Georgia football teams on November 28, 1895, at Piedmont Park, Atlanta. *From* SEC Football: 75 Years of Pride & Passion, *Fred. L. Howe.*

Left: Clemson Tigers football team, 1903. Heisman is in the back row, second from left. *From* The Oconeean, *Clemson University.*

to three consecutive undefeated seasons between 1915 and 1917. While at Georgia Tech, he also invented many of what are considered today to be mainstays of football.

During the 1905 season, eighteen young men were killed while playing college football. In order to reduce injury and fatality for what was, and is, only a game, Heisman helped legalize the forward pass and introduced the quarter system to ensure rest and safety. In addition to these changes, Heisman also created the center snap when his quarterback was too tall to pick the ball off the ground (1893), the lateral pass (1899), the scoreboard (to stop spectators from walking onto the field), the "hike," pads and the overtime system (1922).

After his marriage to his first wife, Evelyn McCollum, dissolved in 1920, Heisman moved on from Georgia Tech and returned to the University of

Pennsylvania. While there, he married his college sweetheart, Edith Cole, with whom he spent the rest of his life. Near the end of his life, Heisman was the athletic director of the Downtown Athletic Club in New York City. The club wanted to give a national Player of the Year award to the best college football player, voted on by sports journalists. While he opposed it at first because he did not like the idea of an individual award for a team sport, Heisman eventually came around.

The trophy was called the Downtown Athletic Club Award and was given to the best player of good character, selfless attitude and good academic standing. It was designed, shaped and cast by twenty-three-year-old Pratt Institute graduate Frank Eliscu in the shape of a player sidestepping and strong-arming a tackler. It was first awarded to University of Chicago halfback Jay Berwanger on December 9, 1935. He was the only player to ever receive the award.

On October 3, 1936, John Heisman died of pneumonia at the age of sixty-six. In the days after his death, the award was renamed the Heisman Trophy and has been given out to the best player in college football every year.

Heisman has been honored in his boyhood home multiple times. On August 31, 1984, a stone monument and plaque were placed in his honor at the corner of the field near his childhood residence where the Titusville Middle School now stands. On August 28, 2009, a Pennsylvania Historic and Museum Commission historical marker was placed above Carter Field, where Heisman played football as a teenager. The young man with pointy ears, a crooked nose, deep-set eyes and a stern mouth grew up in the Oil Region of Pennsylvania playing a game that held little resemblance to the football we know and love today. A hardscrabble life in Northwestern Pennsylvania shaped the man who would become one of the most influential figures in football history.

THE PONTIACS: BLACK BASEBALL PIONEERS IN ERIE, PENNSYLVANIA

Long before Jackie Robinson broke the color barrier of Major League Baseball in 1947, Erie crowds clamored to see the local African American baseball team, the Pontiacs. The Pontiac baseball team was originally formed as a Sunday school church team and was called the St. James AME (African Methodist Episcopal) baseball team.

As the team and its popularity grew, its name changed to the Gem City Monarchs, then to the Flanders Barbers and then to the Empire Athletic Club. The team changed names so many times because every time a new person or group became the major funder, they would change the team's name. Finally, the name changed for the last time to the Pontiacs in 1936 after mail carrier Percival Williams and Ernest Dance approached Carl Longnecker, owner of Longnecker's Pontiac, to sponsor the team. Thus, the mascot was named after the dealership, and the Pontiacs were officially born.

When the Pontiacs played at Bayview Park, they drew crowds of thousands of people. Families knew that they had to show up to the park early to get a seat because by the time the game started, it would be standing room only. The Pontiacs were the talk of the town.

The first Pontiac team in 1936 boasted Edwin A. Roston at third base, Green at second base, Manus at centerfield and as pitcher, Gresham at first base, Holden at left field, Williams at shortstop, West in center field, Dandridge at right field, Harris as pitcher and Welsh at first base. Glaudius "Claudius" Harris was also the most famous manager of the Pontiacs. He guided the team through many tough financial and prejudicial times and came out strong on the other side.

The Pontiacs traveled throughout Northwestern Pennsylvania, playing other small-town, mostly white teams. They widened their scope and also played teams in New York and Ohio, becoming one of the most popular teams in the Glenwood League. Still, they relied on donations from fans and attendees to stay afloat financially. Some regular attendees would even pass around hats requesting donations so that they could come back next week and see their team play again.

In the early 1940s, the Pontiacs were expelled from the Glenwood League for walking off the field before the end of the game. They were picked up by the Lake Shore League and played games in Mill Village, Blooming Valley and Little Hope, Pennsylvania; Sherman, Mayville and Westfield, New York; and Cleveland, Ohio. In 1945, they were brought back into the Glenwood League after immense public outcry that the league was not the same without them and the people of Erie missed watching their games.

Since African Americans were not accepted onto Major League Baseball teams at the time, the Negro League was created so that black players still had the opportunity to show their skills and live out their dreams of being professional baseball players. The Cleveland Buckeyes were a member of the Negro League and were owned by Ernie Wright Sr., an Erie native who grew up at the Pope Hotel in the city. Jessie Pope and her husband, William, established the Pope Hotel in 1928, and her son, Ernie Wright, took over the business in 1933. After his mother died in 1942, Wright became the owner of the Pope Hotel.

In 1945, the Cleveland Buckeyes won the Negro League World Series against the Pittsburgh Homestead Grays. The team was so good that they even challenged the all-white Cleveland Indians, but the Major League Baseball team declined. Shortly after, Wright hired a local Erie girl and daughter of Pontiac third baseman Edwin A. Roston as his secretary. Alice Roston Carter met and befriended a number of Negro League players who would become Pontiac players. Roston Carter wrote in her memoir that it took her a long time to realize how lucky she was to know some of the greatest baseball players of all time, including Sam Jethroe, Willie Grace, Willie Mays, Satchel Paige, W.C. Crosby, George Jefferson, Larry Doby, Josh Gibson, Quincy Trouppe, Archie Ware, Don Bankhead and Monte Irvin, "just to mention a few." She described how players would go multiple nights without sleep because of having to play in double-headers with night games.

African American baseball players were often forced to rent ballparks from white teams while the white teams were playing away games in order to have a place to play. Even if they were able to rent the ballpark, they were rarely, if ever, allowed to use the locker rooms or showers. Prejudice and racism were alive and well in baseball, regardless of talent, kindness or humanity.

On April 25, 1947, twenty-eight-year-old Jackie Robinson took the field with the Brooklyn Dodgers as the first African American to play in Major League Baseball. With his breaking of the baseball color barrier, the Negro Leagues went defunct, and players began trying out and being accepted onto Major League teams. Not all of the former Negro League players were being accepted, however. Many members of the Cleveland Buckeyes joined the Pontiac baseball team in Erie, Pennsylvania.

Willie Grace, Jessie Jethroe, Sam Jethroe, George Jefferson, Willie Jefferson, John Huntley, George Minor and George "Chippy" Britton all moved to Erie so they could continue playing professional baseball. Arguably the most famous new member of the Pontiacs was Sam Jethroe. Sam "The Jet" Jethroe was a center-fielder born in East St. Louis, Illinois, in 1918. He was known for his great speed and leading the league anywhere he played in bases stolen. After winning the Negro League title in 1945, he tried out for the Boston Red Sox along with Marvin Williams and Jackie Robinson. All three black players were turned away. In 1949, Jethroe finally made an

MLB roster and played for the Boston Braves, being named League Rookie of the Year in 1950.

After his retirement from Major League Baseball in 1954, he moved back to Erie and played in the Glenwood League while opening Jethroe's Steak House. In 1994, he sued the MLB for a pension, arguing that his time in the Negro League should count for his retirement since he was actively trying out for Major League teams and turned away because of his race. He lost the suit. Finally, in 1997, the MLB decided to give pensions to former Negro League players who played at least four years in either the Negro League alone or combined with time in the Major League. By that time, Sam Jethroe was almost eighty years old.

On June 18, 2001, Sam Jethroe died in Erie. He has been honored with a bronze plaque at UPMC Park, home of the Erie Seawolves, and remains one of the best baseball players to ever exhibit their prowess in Erie, Pennsylvania.

The Pontiac baseball team provided an opportunity for African American men to rebelliously play the game they loved in the face of racism and prejudice that repeatedly told them that the color of their skin made them unworthy of the opportunity their white counterparts were allowed. Negro League and Glenwood League baseball was a tremendous part of community entertainment and sports history in Northwestern Pennsylvania. The African American Pontiac baseball team existed until 1956, when the team demographics shifted away from a majority of black players. The Pontiac baseball team of Erie, Pennsylvania, made it so that all Americans, regardless of the color of their skin, could make their names as excellent practitioners of America's favorite pastime.

Tenny "The Swayback": Erie's Underdog Champion

One of the most heart-pounding, adrenaline-inducing races in sports history featured a character born and bred in Northwestern Pennsylvania. Unlike the sporting stories told before, this story's protagonist is a chestnut brown, unfortunate-looking fellow who was born along the Erie bayfront and destined for fame. People factor into his rise, but no one person forms the core of his success, for the fellow in this story is Tenny the racehorse.

William Lawrence Scott, Pennsylvania congressman and the first owner of Tenny the racehorse. *From* Virginia Genealogies: A Genealogy of the Glassell Family of Scotland and Virginia *by Reverend Horace Edwin Hayden, 1891.*

Tenny was born in 1886 on the Algeria Farm in Erie, Pennsylvania. The Algeria Farm was owned by millionaire businessman William L. Scott, who was born in Virginia in 1828 and came to Erie as a young man. He was a savvy businessman, becoming the president of the Erie and Pittsburgh Railroad, and soon started his career in politics. Political office made William L. Scott into a household name. He was first elected as mayor of Erie in 1866 and repeated the feat in 1871. Fourteen years later, he ran and was elected as a Democrat in the United States House of Representatives, where he served from 1885 to 1889. Scott was good friends with President Grover Cleveland and was said to be the wealthiest member of the House of Representatives.

With his growing fortune, Scott invested in his passion project of horseracing and breeding. He set up farms in Virginia and Pennsylvania. His Erie farm, Algeria, acted as the stud farm, and many racehorses were sired there. The farm was located just south of Eighth Street and extended to the bayfront and stretched between Beverly Place and Peninsula Road.

One of Scott's first horses was Algerine. Algerine was foaled in Virginia in 1873 and became one of Scott's biggest claims to fame in horseracing. Algerine did not race as a two-year-old and instead made his debut at the Preakness Stakes in 1876. Running with Shirley and Rappahannock, Algerine ran well and came in third. Scott raced Algerine again at the Belmont Stakes soon after. The racehorse Fiddlesticks was the favorite, as he had won the Withers Stakes previously. Algerine beat Fiddlesticks with a time of 2:40:50 and was crowned the Belmont champion. After retiring, Algerine sired many winners. Scott was not yet satisfied.

In the 1880s, Scott wanted to improve his racehorse stock and made waves in the racing world with his purchase of Rayon d'Or ("Ray of Gold") for $40,000. Rayon d'Or was foaled in France in 1876 and won more than fifteen stakes races across Europe. Scott described him as "probably the most magnificent specimen of his race ever imported." After his retirement, Rayon d'Or sired scores of offspring with a variety of different mares. One foal in particular was destined to star in one of the hottest racing events of the nineteenth century.

In 1886, Rayon d'or and Belle of Maywood foaled a small horse named Tenny. With his mixed French and Kentucky ancestry, breeders were expecting Rayon d'Or and Belle of Maywood's offspring to be prime racing material. However, one look at Tenny had Algeria Farm workers shaking their heads in embarrassment.

At birth, it was immediately noted how "deformed and undersized" Tenny appeared. At his first birthday, the farm veterinarian declared that Tenny was a hopeless cause and could never be a racehorse and therefore should be euthanized.

Instead of euthanizing poor Tenny, farm workers instead used him as the butt of their joke. A shipment of horses was being sent east to a buyer. So, as a prank on the purchaser, Algeria farm workers stuck Tenny in the back of the shipment and sent him along too. Upon opening the shipment, the new buyers were furious at this weak runt being dropped on them unannounced and unrequested. At a loss for what else to do and apparently in an attempt at furthering the jest, the new owners put Tenny into training.

TENNY,
BY RAYON D'OR – DAM BELLE OF MAYWOOD.

Currier & Ives image of Tenny the racehorse standing alone, 1891. *Library of Congress.*

While the new owners were preparing to have their fun at Tenny's expense, the horse had other plans. Although he was described as "a pathetic looking little figure with…spindly legs and back that sagged way down in the middle," Tenny was determined to prove to the world that he was worth more than their meanspirited jabs and jokes.

Immediately at the start of his training, Tenny showed amazing potential. His "gameness and tremendous speed were apparent from the start," and he began winning races consistently. The more Tenny won, the more fame he acquired. Crowds loved to watch "The Swayback" race and rooted passionately for the underdog. The more Tenny won, the less he was the underdog, and soon he gained the reputation as one of the best racing horses of the late 1880s.

Alongside Tenny's rise was another magnificent horse: Salvator. Salvator was considered a superhorse, owned by James Ben Ali Haggin. During their third competition season in 1889, Tenny was said to be the only horse with a chance to dethrone Salvator. They finally faced each other at the Realization Stakes, where Salvator won and Tenny came a close second. This meeting was not to be their last.

In their fourth season, Tenny came out swinging, winning four races in a row, while Salvator's owners sat him on the sidelines. Then, in the Suburban Handicap, Haggin finally raced Salvator against a much more tired Tenny; unsurprisingly, Salvator won. Tenny's owner, D.T. Pulsifer, was enraged by the competitor's tactic. In an attempt to get even, Pulsifer challenged Haggin to a head-to-head mile-and-a-quarter race at Sheepshead Bay. Haggin accepted. The stage was set, and the players were anxious to battle it out in front of thousands of roaring fans.

On June 25, 1890, Salvator and Tenny entered their gates in a race for the ages. The Sheepshead Bay track at Coney Island Jockey Course in Sheepshead, New York, was crawling with fans rooting for both horses. Tenny was jockeyed by Snapper Garrison and Salvator by Isaac Murphy, two of the best jockeys of their time—neither was accustomed to losing. The crowd was tense, and the horses were anxious to leap forward into the fray.

Finally, the race began, and both horses bounded forward onto the track. An onlooker described the race: "They ran side by side for the first three furlongs, and then Murphy sent Salvator to the front into the first turn. He outsprinted Tenny down the backstretch and led by three lengths at the head of the stretch. But the dead-game Tenny came on like a demon, overhauling Salvator with every stride." Although Salvator was the stronger racer, Tenny

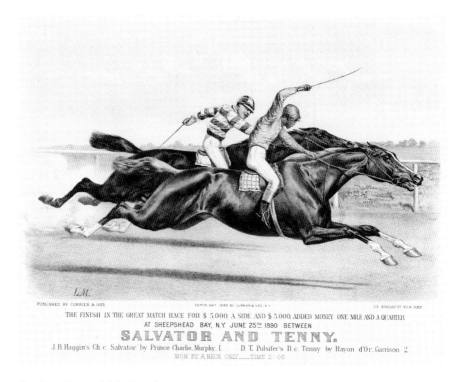

Currier & Ives published this image from the infamous race between Tenny and Salvator at Sheepshead Bay, 1890. *Library of Congress.*

was not ready to give up. He began closing the gap between them until less and less daylight could squeeze between the bodies of the two horses. As they rounded the final curve, the two sprinters were almost even, rushing toward the finish.

Poet Ella Wheeler Wilcox described the final moments of the race:

> *The first mile is covered, the race is mine—no!*
> *For the blue blood of Tenny responds to a blow.*
> *He shoots through the air like a ball from a gun,*
> *And the two lengths between us are shortened to one.*
> *My heart is contracted, my throat feels a lump,*
> *For Tenny's long neck is at Salvator's rump;*
> *And now with new courage, grown bolder and bolder,*
> *I see him once more running shoulder to shoulder.*

As the two horses and their jockeys turned for home, stride for stride, the screaming crowd greeted them and urged both horses to the finish. Salvator and Tenny crossed the finish line beside each other, both confident of victory. Even the jockeys admitted that each thought he had won as they cooled off their horses and trotted around the track. Finally, the crowd and jockeys were informed that in a record-setting time of two minutes and five seconds, one horse had edged the other by no more than a nose—Salvator was victorious. There were mixed cheers and boos from the crowd. No matter which side a fan was on, the consensus was immense pride for Tenny, "The Swayback" from Erie, Pennsylvania, in almost taking down one of the best racehorses of their generation and creating himself a legacy as one of the most inspiring underdogs horseracing has ever had the privilege to experience.

CONCLUSION

Take a breath. Soak it in. Step out from the dust and adrenaline, the horror and passion, the work, play and struggle. Life in Northwestern Pennsylvania was anything but boring or drab. Fast-paced, exciting, heartrending and marked by instances of exquisite love, it is place like so many others and yet wholly its own.

There is so much left to be illuminated in the nooks and crannies of hidden history in this corner of Pennsylvania. We have exposed but a small portion of the crime, disaster, unusualness, industry and life the area has offered for centuries. By thriving in an area so steeped with the vivacity of our collective ancestors, we are living beacons of our history. As time marches on, the questions about our past only continue to grow. Together, we will find the answers and uncover the stories of this small corner of William Penn's wilderness. Stories that will never be forgotten, for they live inside us all.

Bibliography

Chapter 1

1880 U.S. Census. United States Government, 1880.

1870 U.S. Census. United States Government, 1870.

Hatters Friedman, Susan, and Phillip J. Resnick. "Child Murder by Mothers: Patterns and Prevention." *World Psychiatry* 6, no. 3 (October 2007): 137–41.

Mayo Clinic. "Postpartum Depression—Symptoms and Causes," July 29, 2018. http://www.mayoclinic.org/diseases-conditions/postpartum-depression/symptoms-causes/syc-20376617.

Resnick, Phillip J. "Filicide in the United States." *Indian Journal of Psychiatry* 58 (December 2016): S203–9. https://doi.org/10.4103/0019-5545.196845.

Titusville Herald. February 5, 1876.

———. February 9, 1876.

———. February 7, 1876.

———. October 5, 1876.

———. October 3, 1874.

———. September 8, 1874.

———. September 21, 1874.

Chapter 2

Carney, John G. *Tales of Old Erie*. Erie, PA, 1958.

Erie Morning Dispatch. "Sackcloth & Ashes." September 15, 1886.

———. "Silver Creek Disaster." September 18, 1886.

———. "Silver Creek Disaster." September 16, 1886.

———. "Silver Creek Disaster." September 23, 1886.

A Genealogical Tour of Crawford County, Pennsylvania. "Inquests 1862–1875."
   July 29, 2018. http://www.crawfordcopa.com/court/inquest/1862-75.html.

Haine, Edgar A. *Railroad Wrecks*. Plainsboro, NJ: Associated University Presses, 1993.

New York Times. "The Silver Creek Disaster." September 17, 1886.

Peet, Reverend Stephen D. *The Ashtabula Disaster*. Chicago, IL: J.S. Goodman, 1877.

Titusville Herald. December 30, 1876.

———. January 1, 1877.

———. January 3, 1877.

———. January 31, 1877.

———. January 12, 1877.

Chapter 3

Abbott, Karen. "The Fox Sisters and the Rap on Spiritualism." *Smithsonian Magazine*,
   October 30, 2012. https://www.smithsonianmag.com/history/the-fox-sisters-
   and-the-rap-on-spiritualism-99663697.

Bates, Samuel. *History of Crawford County, Pennsylvania*. Chicago: Warner, Beers &
   Company, 1885.

Bradford Era. February 26, 1889.

Caligraph Quarterly 1, no. 4 (December 1883).

Deegan, John A. *Pennsylvania State Hospital System Length-of-Stay, Demographics, and
   Diagnoses Report for December 31, 2014*. Wernersville: Pennsylvania Department
   of Human Services Office of Mental Health and Substance Abuse Services,
   February 2015. http://dhs.pa.gov/cs/groups/webcontent/documents/
   report/c_149849.pdf.

Gregory, Candace. "A Willing Suspension of Disbelief: Victorian Reaction to the
   Spiritual Phenomena." *Student Historical Journal* 21, no. 90 (1989).

Kirkbride, Thomas Story. *On the Construction, Organization, and General Arrangement of
   Hospitals for the Insane*. Philadelphia, PA, 1854.

Messenger, Robert. "On This Day in Typewriter History (XCIX)." *Oz. Typewriter*
   (blog), August 28, 2011. https://oztypewriter.blogspot.com/2011/08/on-this-
   day-in-typewriter-history-xcix.html.

———. "On This Day in Typewriter History (XXI)." *Oz. Typewriter* (blog), June 10,
   2011. https://oztypewriter.blogspot.com/2011/06/on-this-day-in-typewriter-
   history-xxi.html.

New York Times. September 30, 1895.

Notzing, Baron Albert Von Schrenck. *Phenomena of Materialisation: A Contribution to the Investigation of Mediumistic Teleplastics*. New York: E.P. Dutton and Company, 1920.

Pithole Daily Record. August 8, 1866.

————. January 24, 1866.

————. March 14, 1866.

Pitman, Sir Isaac. *Pitman's Journal of Commercial Education*. London: Isaac Pitman & Sons, 1892.

Stamp, Jimmy. "Fact of Fiction? The Legend of the QWERTY Keyboard." *Smithsonian*, May 3, 3013. https://www.smithsonianmag.com/arts-culture/fact-of-fiction-the-legend-of-the-qwerty-keyboard-49863249.

Titusville Herald. April 9, 1921.

————. April 20, 1905.

————. April 22, 1896.

————. August 16, 1919.

————. December 2, 1921.

————. February 19, 1879.

————. February 25, 2016.

————. January 25, 1866.

————. January 24, 1866.

————. January 22, 1866.

————. January 27, 1897.

————. January 27, 1866.

————. January 26, 1866.

————. January 23, 1866.

————. June 30, 1896.

————. March 28, 1889.

————. November 15, 1880.

————. October 16, 1915.

————. October 25, 1915.

————. September 19, 1930.

————. September 12, 1914.

————. September 21, 1900.

————. September 26, 1882.

Wade, Joseph Marshall. *Posthumous Memoirs of Helena Petrovna Blavatsky*. Boston: Jos. M. Wade, 1896.

Warren Ledger. May 11, 1888.

Warren Mail. January 27, 1874.

————. October 12, 1880.

Warren Mirror. August 6, 1888.

Yanni, Carla. *The Architecture of Madness: Insane Asylums in the United States.* Minneapolis: University of Minnesota Press, 2007.

Chapter 4

Bush, Lee O., and Richard F. Hershey. *Conneaut Lake Park: The First 100 Years of Fun.* Fairview Park, OH: Amusement Park Books, 1992.

Conneaut Lake Park. "Rides." http://www.newconneautlakepark.com/attractions/rides.cfm.

Costello, Michael E. *Conneaut Lake Park.* Charleston, SC: Arcadia Publishing, 2005.

Currie, Harold W. *Eugene V. Debs.* Boston: Twayne Publishers, 1976.

Cyclops Steel Company. *Fifty Years of Progress, 1884–1934.* Titusville, PA: Cyclops Steel Company, 1934.

———. *Specialty Steelmaking Pioneers, 1884.* Titusville, PA: Cyclops Steel Company, 1984.

GoErie. "Fire Damages Former Marx Toys Plant." July 13, 2016.

Grygier, Nanette T. "Eastern European Migration to Northwest Pennsylvania: A Case Study of Crossingville, Pennsylvania." Master's thesis, Edinboro University of Pennsylvania, 2004.

Lawrence County Historical Society. "New Castle." County Historical Society. https://www.lawrencechs.com/museum/exhibits/new-castle.

Magocsi, Paul R. *Our People: Carpatho-Rusyns and Their Descendants in North America.* Mundelein, IL: Bolchazy-Carducci Publishers, 2005.

New Castle News. "Tyler Elected." November 8, 1911.

Pinsky, Maxine A. *Marx Toys: Robots, Space, Comic, Disney, and TV Characters.* Atglen, PA: Schiffer Publishing, 1996.

Pittsburgh Gazette Times. "Socialist Rally." May 2, 1915.

Pittsburgh Press. "Conneaut Lake Encampment." June 20, 1915.

———. "Tent Rental." March 21, 1915.

Radosh, Ronald. *Debs.* Upper Saddle River, NJ: Prentice-Hall, 1971.

Reed, Irene, ed. *Berks County Women in History: Profiles.* Vol. 1. Leesport, PA: Tudor Gate Press, 2005.

Rise and Fall of a Tin Toy Dynasty. Documentary. Erie, PA: WQLN, November 17, 1991.

Saints Peter and Paul Orthodox Church. "History of the Patriarchal Parishes in the USA." The Patriarchal Parishes in the USA: Moscow Patriarchate. https://orthodoxcrossingville.org/parishdeclaration.html.

————. "Parish Declaration." https://orthodoxcrossingville.org/parishdeclaration. html.

Sekel, Nicholas. Interview on early Carpatho-Rusyn life in Northwestern Pennsylvania. Interview by Jessica Hilburn, September 4, 2018.

St. Nicholas Orthodox Church. "About the Parish." https://orthodoxcrossingville. org/parishdeclaration.html.

Titusville Herald. August 21, 2014.

————. "Interesting Debate Held." September 9, 1908.

————. September 20, 1984.

————. September 21, 1984.

————. "Socialist Chautauqua at Exposition Park." June 10, 1915.

————. "Socialist Debate to Be Held." September 7, 1908.

————. "Socialists Preparing Big Meeting." August 23, 1910.

Warzeski, Walter C. *Byzantine Rite Rusins in Carpatho-Ruthenia and America*. Pittsburgh, PA: Byzantine Seminary Press, 1971.

Washington Observer-Reporter. February 1, 1973.

Weber, David L. *Around Titusville*. Charleston, SC: Arcadia Publishing, 2004.

Chapter 5

Bemis, Jan. *Corry*. Charleston, SC: Arcadia Publishing, 2012.

Cambridge Springs Heritage Society. *A History of the Riverside Inn: Cambridge Springs, PA*. Cambridge Springs, PA: self-published, 2017.

Cutter, Charles. *Cutter's Guide to Cambridge Springs, the Great Health and Pleasure Resort of Pennsylvania*. N.p.: Charles Cutter & Son, 1902.

Pharmaceutical Era. Detroit, MI: D.O. Haynes & Company, 1892.

Philadelphia Times. "Corry Artesian Mineral Water Company." March 17, 1896.

Titusville Herald. April 8, 1914.

————. August 17, 1977.

————. August 30, 2005.

————. January 29, 1906.

————. January 23, 1947.

————. June 14, 1990.

————. June 17, 1907.

————. June 16, 1951.

Chapter 6

Allen, Cain. "Modoc War." The Oregon History Project, 2013. https://oregonhistoryproject.org/articles/historical-records/modoc-war/#.W576Z OhKhPY.

Bates, Samuel. *Our County and Its People.* Boston: W.A. Fergusson, 1889.

Bradford Era. May 27, 1908.

Burczyk, Martha Ruth. *Warren.* Charleston, SC: Arcadia Publishing, 2010.

Cotton, Josh. "Piso's Cure for Consumption." *Warren Times Observer,* November 11, 2017.

Fowler, Gene, and Marshall Wyatt. "Days & Nights at the Physic Opera." *Cowboys and Indians Magazine* (2014). https://www.cowboysindians.com/2014/09/days-nights-at-the-physic-opera.

Hilburn, Juliet, and Jessica Hilburn. "Ridgway Cemetery." Ridgway Cemetery. https://ridgwaycemetery.org.

Hirschfelder, Arlene B., and Paulette Fairbanks Molin. *The Extraordinary Book of Native American Lists.* Lanham, MD: Scarecrow Press, 2012.

Jette, Melinda. "Donald McKay." The Oregon History Project. https://oregonhistoryproject.org/articles/historical-records/donald-mckay/#.W576XuhKhPY.

McNamara, Brooks. "The Indian Medicine Show." *Educational Theatre Journal* 23, no. 4 (December 1971): 431–45. https://doi.org/10.2307/3205750.

New Bethlehem Vindicator. August 8, 1902.

Ridgway, Harry. *Titusville Herald.* August 19, 1949.

———. *Titusville Herald.* August 26, 1949.

———. *Titusville Herald.* September 2, 1949.

Ridgway, Samuel. *Ridgway Sanitarium: Its Description and Growth.* Pamphlet. Hydetown, PA, 1897.

———. "Ridgway's Acme Liniment." United States Patent Office 3341. Hydetown, PA, issued July 3, 1883.

Smethport McKean Democrat. March 17, 1899.

Sullivan, Jack. "Piso's Trio: One Step Ahead of the Law." *Bottles and Extras,* October 2007.

Titusville Herald. April 3, 1947.

———. April 28, 1896.

———. December 14, 1903.

———. December 16, 1892.

———. December 31, 1895.

———. February 8, 1901.

———. January 16, 1919.

————. July 29, 1911.

————. May 5, 1892.

————. May 4, 1892.

————. October 2, 1903.

————. October 7, 1907.

————. September 8, 1900.

United States Food and Drug Administration. *Notices of Judgment Under the Food and Drugs Act*. 5501st ed. Washington, D.C.: U.S. Government Printing Office, 1916.

Vogel, Virgil J. *American Indian Medicine*. Norman: University of Oklahoma Press, 2013.

Warren Evening Mirror. November 15, 1911.

Warren Evening Times. August 22, 1915.

————. October 23, 1916.

Warren Ledger. January 5, 1892.

Warren Mail. April 28, 1904.

————. November 28, 1894.

————. October 14, 1891.

————. October 20, 1910.

————. October 23, 1895.

————. "Woman Suicides for Love of a Dashing Showman." November 2, 1888.

Wellsville Allegany County Democrat. May 18, 1892.

Chapter 7

Boukari, Safoura. "20th Century Black Women's Struggle for Empowerment in a White Supremacist Educational System: Tribute to Early Women Educators." University of Nebraska–Lincoln, 2005.

Burczyk, Martha Ruth. *Warren*. Charleston, SC: Arcadia Publishing, 2010.

Burdick, Jonathan. "Erie's Historical Women." *Erie Reader*, November 8, 2017.

Domowicz, Geoffrey L. *Girard: A Canal Town History*. Charleston, SC: Arcadia Publishing, 2003.

Eiler, Linda Lee Hessong. *Girard*. Charleston, SC: Arcadia Publishing, 2005.

Erie Times-News. "Ada Lawrence Obituary." March 11, 2014. http://www.legacy. com/obituaries/erietimesnews/obituary.aspx?n=ada-louise-lawrence&pid=170 112357&fhid=8452.

Freeman, Sabina Shields, and Margaret L. Tenpas. *Erie History: The Women's Story*. Erie, PA: Benet Press for Erie, Pennsylvania Branch, American Association of University Women, 1982.

Goldin, Claudia. "Female Labor Force Participation: The Origin of Black and White Differences, 1870 and 1880." *Journal of Economic History* 37, no. 1 (1977): 87–108.

Houseman, Adriana. *African Americans in Erie County: A Heritage Trail.* Brochure, Mercyhurst University, Erie, Pennsylvania, 2012. https://www.mercyhurst.edu/sites/default/files/uploads/brochure.pdf.

Thompson, Sarah S. *Journey from Jerusalem: An Illustrated Introduction to Erie's African American History, 1795–1995.* Erie, PA: Erie County Historical Society, 1996.

Titusville Herald. January 16, 1919.

Warren Evening Mirror. December 7, 1917.

———. December 6, 1917.

———. December 3, 1917.

Warren Morning Chronicle. January 7, 1919.

Chapter 8

Carter, Alice Roston. *Can I Get a Witness?: Growing Up in the Black Middle Class in Erie, Pennsylvania.* Erie, PA: Erie County Historical Society, 1991.

Cuneo, Kevin. "Sam Jethroe Still Remembered in Erie." *GoErie*, April 6, 2017.

Daily Alta California. "Salvator Tenny Race." August 13, 1890.

Ella Wheeler Wilcox Society. "How Salvator Won." Poem, 1892. http://www.ellawheelerwilcox.org/poems/phowsal2.htm.

Goldberg, Ryan. "The Golden Era of Brooklyn Racing." *Daily Racing Form*, August 8, 2018. http://www.drf.com/news/golden-era-brooklyn-racing.

Heisman, John M., and Mark Schlabach. *Heisman: The Man Behind the Trophy.* New York: Simon & Schuster, 2012.

Moore, Larry W. *The Pontiacs: Black Baseball to Remember.* Erie, PA: Larry W. Moore, 2010.

Thompson, Sarah S., and Karen James. *Journey from Jerusalem: An Illustrated Introduction to Erie's African American History, 1795–1995.* Erie, PA: Erie County Historical Society, 1996.

Whipple, Frank B. *Algeria Stud Farm, Property of W.L. Scott, Erie, Pa.* Erie, PA: Herald Printing and Publishing Company, 1889. http://archive.org/details/algeriastudfarmp00whip.

INDEX